# HOW THE
# FUTURES
# MARKETS
## WORK

Jake Bernstein
New York Institute of Finance

Bernstein, Jacob, 1946-
    How the futures markets work / Jake Bernstein.
        p.    cm.
    Includes index.
    ISBN 0-13-407222-7 :
    1. Futures market.    I. New York Institute of Finance.    II. Title.
HG6024.A3B49    1989
332.64'4--dc19                                          89-3220
                                                           CIP

This publication is designed to provide accurate and authoritative information in regard to the subject matter covered. It is sold with the understanding that the publisher is not engaged in rendering legal, accountin,g or other professional service. If legal advice or other expert assistance is required, the services of a competent professional person should be sought.

*From a Declaration of Principles Jointly Adopted by a Committee of the American Bar Association and a Committee of Publishers and Associations*

Printed in the United States of America

10  9  8  7  6  5


New York Institute of Finance
(NYIF Corp.)
70 Pine Street
New York, New York 10270-0003

# Contents

. . . Contract Months . . . Placing an Order . . .
Types of Orders . . . Commissions . . . Day Trading
Versus Position Trading . . . Hedging . . . Spreads
and Straddles . . . Trading Spreads . . . Margin
Requirements with Spreads . . . Commissions on
Spreads . . . Market Research and Study . . . Market
Entry and Exit . . . Spreads as an Index to Market
Behavior . . . Sample Spread Charts . . . Futures
Options Trading . . . Margin in Options Trading . . .
Exit Alternatives . . . Advantages of Options Trading
. . . Disadvantages of Options Trading . . . Strategies
for Trading Options . . . Regulatory Agencies . . .
National Futures Association . . . Who Must Register
with the CFTC?

CHAPTER 7
## *Fundamental Forces on the Market, 127*

Supply and Demand . . . Market Reports . . .
Seasonality . . . Seasonal Tendencies in Futures Prices
. . . Cyclic Price Changes . . . Secular Trends . . .
Government Price Support . . . Government Reports
. . . Political Decisions . . . Weather . . .
International News . . . Fluctuation of the Dollar . . .
General Business Conditions . . . Price Analysis

CHAPTER 8
## *The Basics of Technical Analysis, 149*

Charts . . . The Bar Chart . . . The Point-and-Figure
Chart . . . Chart Patterns . . . Trends . . . Reversal
Patterns . . . Timing of Trades . . . Moving Averages
. . . Using the Moving Average . . . Multiple Moving
Averages . . . Variations on the Moving Average . . .
Conclusions About Moving Averages . . . Oscillators
. . . Relative Strength Index . . . Stochastics . . .
Other Oscillators . . . Volume and Open Interest . . .
The Wave Theories . . . Fibonacci Number Series

# *What This Book Can Do for You*

Futures trading is, in many respects, one of the last frontiers of capitalism. It is one of the few remaining investment-related vehicles requiring relatively low capital input that can, with motivation, persistence, and skill, offer virtually unlimited profit potential. Much has been said about the moneymaking potential of real estate investing. And there is, no doubt, much promise in such speculations or investments as land, income properties, tax delinquent properties, mortgage default properties, contract buying, and a host of relatively new as well as time-tested approaches. It is virtually impossible nowadays to watch a late-night television show without being exposed to an onslaught of advertisements and/or "talk" shows promoting a wide selection of programs, courses, books, and other plans for profiting from real estate investments and/or speculations. Although there may be much truth and potential in such schemes, there are few investors who have the discipline, motivation, or resources to follow through on these programs with the consistency required for success. Those who do achieve success following such programs are likely to represent a very small minority. Yet this situation is not unique to the area of real estate investing or speculation. There is virtually no human endeavor—personal, academic, professional, or business-related—that can succeed without the prerequisite elements of discipline, knowledge, motivation, consistency, and persistence.

Although there has been considerably less media attention to the area of futures trading and speculation, it is a fact that there are few capitalist ventures that are either as speculative, promising, misunderstood, maligned, risky, or as basic as is futures trading. Those of us who have been involved in the futures industry for many years know that, on the surface, the "game" seems simple, offers the promise of virtually unlimited wealth, and requires only a minimum in start-up capital. This is at one and the same time the lure as well as the danger of futures trading. Those of us who have traded futures for many years also know that it is impossible to speak of the potential profits without also speaking in even more definitive terms about the potential losses. Although it is true that futures trading can be learned by almost everyone, it is also true that

1. futures trading is not a science;

2. there are no shortcuts or cookbook formulas to success in futures trading;

3. one can lose more than one's original investment or speculative capital in trading the futures markets;

4. there are nine losers for every one winner in the futures markets;

5. lasting success rarely comes quickly or easily; and

6. in spite of its seeming simplicity, futures trading is one of the most difficult and demanding endeavors an individual can assume.

## WHY TRADE FUTURES?

When I first began trading in the futures markets in 1968, my motivation was entirely financial. I was in search of the path to quick riches. I, like so many other newcomers, was motivated by the promise of wealth and the attraction of low starting capital. I realized that futures speculation (or commodity trading as it was then called) was a game that required a minimum of start-up capital, no major investment in equipment, no lease or space requirements (other than perhaps a desk and quotation equipment), and no fixed location from which my work had to be done. I could speculate for the short term, the long term, or the intermediate term. And best of all, I had the potential to use the powerful leverage of the futures markets to my advantage. In other words, the ability to control $50,000 in goods for less than $1,000 in cash outlay was a most attractive proposition. Unfortunately, during those days there were few who warned me about the risks and the very low probability of success. It was not too long after I began my trading career that I realized the odds of success were not at all in my favor. It was not until many years later that I realized how to tilt the odds in my favor and how to rectify many of the errors and loss-producing behaviors that were part of my trading repertoire. It was also unfortunate that my initial venture into speculation met with great success, for it was not until my virtually immediate success turned into abysmal and total failure that I realized the clearly two-sided nature of futures speculation. In view of the attendant risks, stringent discipline, organization, and commitment that futures trading requires, the question naturally arises "Why trade futures?" And it is a good question indeed. It is a question to which cogent and personally meaningful answers must be found before any individual can undertake the task of becoming a futures trader. Perhaps, you will find some meaningful answers listed below:

*1. Futures trading offers the independent individual a career* that can lead to great wealth, provided one is clearly in touch with the underlying risk of loss and one can put forth the effort and discipline necessary to achieve the promised success.

*2. The futures industry is growing rapidly. There are many career paths to follow.* One need not become an independent speculator if one does not have an interest in or the temperament to pursue independent speculation. Careers in brokerage, market analysis, computerized trading technology, computer software and hardware support, accounting, law, advertising, and other services related to futures trading offer excellent potential. However, you must know and understand the markets before you can follow the course to any of these vocations.

*3. The futures markets are, in many respects, leading economic indicators.* They can tell you many things about the current and projected economic trends. To understand the futures markets and their current status is to understand the economy. And this can be a valuable help in all of your other investments, long term as well as short term.

*4. Learning how to trade futures can help you develop the discipline* necessary in many other investment areas.

*5. And last but certainly not least, the incentive to make profits beginning with a minimal amount of risk capital is one of the most attractive reasons for trading futures.* Yet, paradoxically, it should not be your first or only reason. Profits in futures trading are the outcome of meeting many prerequisite conditions. It is very important not to put the cart before the horse. If you are disciplined, attentive, consistent, and true to your trading system or method, then you will benefit in the long run and profits will be yours. I will discuss this further in the chapters that follow.

## SOME PRELIMINARIES

Before you read on, some preliminary comments about futures trading and about this book are in order. Rather than entering into a dissertation on the topics just mentioned, I will simply enumerate my points. Please read them carefully so that you will not have any prejudices or misconceptions about this book or about futures trading.

1. This book will not provide you with a complete education in futures trading. To cover the topic completely, and to provide you with the necessary skills to trade or to acquire professional certification will require much more reading and/or structured course work.

2. This book can serve only as a starting point. If after reading this book you find that futures trading and/or the futures industry are of interest to you, then there are many avenues you can pursue to further your education. However, do not make the grievous error of thinking that you know all there is to know after you read this book.

3. Should you decide to speculate in the futures market, then remember that futures trading involves the risk of loss as well as the potential for reward. Although profits are alluring, the potential for losing more than your original investment always must be foremost in your mind.

*4.* Because of space limitations, there are many topics that cannot be covered in sufficient detail in this book. Topics that are covered are given only the most elementary discussion. If you are not a newcomer to futures trading, or if you have already been exposed to the basic concepts of futures trading, then this book is not for you.

Finally, a few suggestions that may facilitate your learning follow.

*1. Take notes.* Although I have presented much of the material herein in anecdotal form, I suggest that you extract the basic concepts and make appropriate notes.

*2. If you do not understand a given topic or concepts, please reread them until you do understand them.* If you are still at a loss, then you may wish to consult one of the sources cited in the reading list in the Appendix.

*3. Application of the concepts can assist in your understanding and learning.* Get a copy of the *Wall Street Journal* or *Futures Magazine.* Do some reading. See how well you can understand the futures talk in these publications. You may be pleasantly surprised to see how much you've learned.

*4. Don't be afraid to "get your feet wet"* once you feel confident with your knowledge. However, remember to be conservative and, above all, never to take a risk that you cannot afford.

It is my sincere hope that you will find this book well suited to fulfill the needs you had when you decided to let me be your teacher. Yet, I must hasten to add that the knowledge this book will convey is far from complete, far from sufficient, but certainly more than enough to get you started in the right direction.

Jake Bernstein
MBH Commodity Advisors, Inc.
Northbrook, IL 60062

# The Journey That Awaits You

You are about to embark on a journey that will radically and beneficially alter your understanding of the so-called "investment" world. Assuming that you know little or nothing about futures trading, and assuming that previously you have formed some conceptions about the nature of speculation and investing, we will begin our journey at an elementary level. Before concentrating on such things as the definition of futures trading, or the organization and structure of the futures markets, there are several more basic conceptual considerations that must be understood. Specifically, these involve both the philosophy and the psychology of speculation and

investing. Without a firm intellectual footing about the aforementioned components of futures trading, our travels will lack depth, true meaning, and direction. So please prepare to abandon some ideas that may have come to you through the educational system, through your own readings, and/or through your own observations. But fear not, I have no intention of stripping away all of your present ideas inasmuch as some of them may, in fact, correlate clearly with what I have to tell you.

## A WORLD OF MISUNDERSTANDING

Language cannot help but bring with it value judgments that are associated with words, their usage, subtle meanings, and even their intonation. Words conjure up mental pictures, some of which bring with them positive thoughts, some which bring neutral thoughts, and others which prompt negative thoughts. Let's consider, for example, the differences between investing, speculating, and gambling. What do you think about when you hear each of these words? What are your mental images of each word? If your thoughts are like those of most people then you may imagine the following:

*Investor:* You picture a well-dressed man, perhaps wearing a three-piece suit, sitting at a large desk, perhaps in a bank, pouring over earnings reports, possibly adding figures on a calculator, or examining stock prices in the *Wall Street Journal.* If you're not oriented to the business world, then you may imagine an everyday person seated in his or her study, analyzing business reports, perhaps looking at stock price charts, or talking to a stockbroker. In any event, your mental picture is likely to attribute the following characteristics to the "investor": some degree of affluence, intelligence, logic, studiousness, organization, skill in selecting investments, discipline, and confidence in varying degrees. Clearly indicative of our preconceptions, many of us would not picture a woman, a very young person, a very old person,

a foreigner, a disorganized individual, or someone who is either uneducated, highly emotional, or poor. There are many other preconceptions or stereotypes that could enter into our initial mental picture of the investor. In reality, there is no investor that fits any one definition particularly well. Investors come from all walks of life, all levels of education, all races, both sexes, and virtually every age group. Yet, it is not possible for the human mind to think in such general terms. We must, therefore, construct, or stereotype a given notion of the investor. This is both good and bad at the same time. It is good because it allows for mental organization, but it is bad inasmuch as it distorts reality. Now let's look at our mental picture of another group.

*Speculator:* When asked to construct a mental image of someone who is a speculator, many of us imagine a middle-aged individual, usually male (perhaps more often so than in the case of the stereotyped investor). We think of an aggressive, more impulsive individual, perhaps on the trading floor of the stock or futures exchange. He might be holding several telephones at once, buying on one telephone while selling on the other.

Many individuals suspect that the "speculator" seeks to capitalize on the fortunes of others, taking advantage of short-term disturbances in the equilibrium of the markets. Generally, the feeling tone attributed by most mental images is one of greed, aggression, and youthful wealth without consideration for the feelings or finances of others. In reality, however, a great majority of speculators do not fall into this stereotypic image. In fact, there may be, as you will see, no adequate or all-encompassing definition of the speculator distinguished from the investor. Now let's look at our mental image of the gambler.

*Gambler:* This group of individuals is held in the lowest of esteem. When we think of the gambler, we often imagine a person driven by a compulsion to "play the horses" or to visit the casinos of Las Vegas. We feel that the gambler must gamble, whether he makes money or not. The gambler is most often perceived to be a man

. . . much more so than the investor or speculator. In our mind's eye, the gambler is suffering from a mental disorder, he may also be prone to excessive use of alcohol or drugs, and he will rarely be a consistent winner. He is most often destined to lose and suffer. We tend to think of gamblers as less educated in comparison to the investor and of the speculator falling somewhere between the gambler and the investor in terms of education, intelligence, and skill. In other words, the common misconception is that it takes skill and intelligence to invest, intuition and brawn to speculate, and greed to gamble. In fact, none of the above is necessarily true.

In addition, it is generally believed that investors are apt to be productive individuals whose involvement in the markets is socially and economically productive, whereas speculators provide little or no economic function and gamblers actually detract from society and the economy by their behavior. In reality, virtually none of the above is true on any consistent or pervasive basis.

The purpose of our little exercise has been to

*1.* Demonstrate that the human mind must, for sake of its own organizationally efficiency and integrity, engage in stereotypical or generalized thinking,

*2.* That such thinking, although necessary on one level, may distort reality, thereby leading to a host of irrational and/or counterproductive behaviors, and

*3.* That what we have been led or educated to believe is not necessarily true, productive, or otherwise beneficial.

If what you have learned about investing—speculating is not based in truth or reality—then you will be prone to make decisions that may affect not only friendships and other relationships but could also significantly impact your career and financial future. If, for example, you've been prone to think of the investor as an individual very much different than yourself in skill, intellect, or social class, then you may mentally close the door to your achievement. You effectively close your mind to the possibility of success as an investor. And in so doing, you do, in fact, close the door, thereby not allowing your mind to prompt behaviors necessary for success in this field. If you think of the speculator as aggressive and quick-witted but of yourself as gentle and methodical, then you rule out the possibility of success as a speculator. If you consider the speculator to be an individual who capitalizes on the misfortune of others but of yourself as a sensitive and caring human being, then you will never allow yourself to venture into an area that could bring you vast fortunes and great excitement. Finally, if you think that speculators and investors are nothing more than erudite gamblers, then you may never allow yourself the opportunity to see what capitalism can do for you.

For many years, I practiced as a clinical psychologist. I worked with patients of every age, ability, social status, and intellectual level. My patients were black, white, Hispanic, Oriental, American Indian, and more. Virtually all religious groups were represented, as were many professions. I learned well that the human mind is the ultimate force behind all action. And, therefore, that the source and motivation of all human achievement is the mind. What we tell ourselves has a direct and even predictable outcome on behavior. Although the implications of this last statement are vast, they are by no means less applicable to the areas of investing and speculating than they are to the area of human psychology and behavior. My point is simply and concisely as follows.

For all too long the role, function, and behavior of investors and speculators have not been well understood. In fact, they have been grossly distorted. This has resulted in the following misconceptions, none of which is always true and all of which tend to dissuade many individuals from following a career in these fields or from assuming a part-time role as an investor or speculator.

Investors in stocks, futures, real estate, or other ventures must begin with considerable capital to achieve financial success. You must have money in order to make money. As a matter of fact, many successful investors began with little or nothing. Their success developed slowly, through great effort, and wise decision making. Failures were frequent, but persistence was eventually victorious.

Futures trading holds the promise of wealth and success, yet it is an endeavor that requires skill, discipline, and persistence. The goal of this book is to provide you with the basic tools you will need to progress through the higher levels of learning that are prerequisite to success in the futures industry. Bear in mind that there are many different facets to the futures markets; that there are many ways in which you can participate. You need not be a speculator . . . you can become a broker, analyst, administrator, or fund-raiser . . . but none of these alternatives will be possible without a solid foundation. Don't let this book be your ending point . . . rather let it be the first step of your journey.

# CHAPTER 2

# What Is a Commodity Futures Contract?

Woody Carver (a fictitious name) is a very talented person. Since he was a very young child he has been able to create delicate, lifelike figures from small bits of wood, using only a set of knives that he inherited from his grandfather, Woodrow Carver I. Woody carves an impressive array of miniature animals and people— squirrels, horses, toy soldiers, and historical personalities. Recently, he began producing miniature wooden versions of exotic cars, which are very popular with some of his professional friends.

A few years ago, Jack Merchant (also a fictitious name) saw some of the marvelous toys that Woody had

created, and he asked Woody if he could offer some of
them for sale in his trendy little boutique at the local
mall. Woody agreed, and the hand-carved figures quickly
became a favorite of Jack's customers, who bought all
of the original consignment within a week, paying very
high prices for them. Jack knew he had something and
asked Woody for more.

Having sold the little toys for far more than he ever
imagined their worth to be (this was, after all, only a
hobby to Woody before Jack came along), Woody excitedly
agreed to sell Jack some more carved figures. This time,
however, he did not have a ready supply, as Jack had
bought most of his collection the first time. So he agreed
to deliver some of the figures immediately and the rest
in two months. By working in the evenings and on
weekends, Woody was able to fulfill his agreement with
Jack, who in turn sold the popular little carvings as
quickly as he put them on display. A number of customers, in fact, began ordering specific figures that they
particularly liked, and Jack in turn began placing orders
with Woody.

To meet the demand for his little creatures, Woody
hired a neighborhood youth to work with him on some
of the simpler models, and he began teaching him the
art of wood carving. Within a year, Woody had quit his
job and was overseeing a work force of five assistants,
three of whom were learning Woody's craft as appren-
tices. Jack, on the other hand, was marketing Woody's
creations through a mail-order catalogue he had established a few months earlier, and the orders were flooding
in. Hundreds of customers wanted toy soldiers for Christ-
mas, while hundreds more were eager to purchase a
miniature Ferrari or Lamborghini. Jack quickly discovered that he should have placed larger orders for certain
items many months ahead of time, as he ran out of some
of the more popular items after filling only a fraction of
the orders.

Realizing that he must plan better for the second
catalogue, Jack met with Woody and they agreed that

Woody's shop, now known as Mini-Carve, would produce 10,000 wooden soldiers by the next September and 5,000 each of the Lamborghini and the Ferrari by the coming July, to be delivered to Jack's warehouse in good condition and of the same quality as Woody's past products. Woody was pleased when Jack paid him 5% of the agreed-upon price as a binder to the deal. Jack was confident that he would make a killing on the resale of Woody's popular handmade toys, judging from the response to the prior catalogue.

Only rarely, usually just before falling asleep, did Jack consider the risk he had taken. After all, he had agreed to pay more money than he could possibly raise for thousands of little toys that might not sell. At those moments, Jack remembered how fickle many of his boutique customers could be. He recalled the few times he had bought large quantities of items that he just knew his clientele would snap up, only to have them sit unsold on his shelf, ultimately to be disposed of to a discount store at a loss.

One day, a few weeks after the signing of the contract with Jack, Woody got a telephone call from Mr. Harvey Watts, who identified himself as the buyer for a huge Midwest mail-order conglomerate. What Harvey wanted to know was, would Woody be interested in selling his carvings through their catalogue, which had a very large distribution and clientele. Woody was flattered but was forced to tell him he already had a delivery contract with Jack Merchant as well as an agreement that Jack would have exclusive distribution rights to his creations.

Upon hearing this news, Mr. Watts called Mr. Merchant to inquire whether Jack might be willing to relinquish his distribution rights and sell the toys he had ordered. "Jack," said Harvey, "how much did you agree to pay for those little hand-carved beauties?"

"Well, Harvey, I have a contract to buy 10,000 toy soldiers in September at a price of $2.00 each and a contract to buy 10,000 wooden cars in July at a cost of $5.00 each."

"Tell you what, Jack, I'll take those contracts off your hands. I'll pay $2.20 for the soldiers and $5.50 for the cars. You get the difference in cash up front."

Jack quickly figured in his head what he could make on this deal. At 20 cents a piece for the toy soldiers, he would receive $2,000, and at 50 cents each for the cars, he would get $5,000. He had already paid Woody $3,500 as earnest money, so he would profit handsomely on his original investment if he sold the contract. On the other hand, he had planned to resell the figures through his own catalogue at a 30% profit, which would net him $21,000. To sell the contract now would deprive him of $14,000 in potential profits. If the items didn't sell, though, he faced a potential $70,000 loss.

"Harvey," Jack said, "I just can't let those little guys go. I really love those little carvings, and so do my customers. My little girl would never forgive me if I sold off my stake in Mini-Carve."

"Jack, I'll give you 20% on each item—40 cents for the soldiers and a buck for the cars—cash up front."

"You got a deal, Harvey."

At that moment, Jack and Harvey completed a transaction involving two futures contracts—contracts established originally between Jack and Woody. Each contract specified that a certain quantity (10,000) of a commodity (hand-carved wooden soldiers and hand-carved wooden cars) would be delivered to a certain place (Jack's warehouse) on a specified date (September and July) in good condition and of the same quality as past toys had been. Because all of these criteria were included in the original contract, it could easily be transferred to a third party (Harvey). Of course, Harvey would probably change the delivery site, but that change would likely cost him additional money in freight charges.

Who benefited from the transactions? Woody, of course, was the beneficiary of a contract that assured him a price for his toys before he ever manufactured them. Thus, he could plan his production and control his costs so as to guarantee himself a profit. He would not have to speculate about the market for his toys several months hence. Thus, he transferred the risk of financial losses to Jack by making the contract with him.

After some initial euphoria, Jack began to realize that he had taken on a lot of risk. He had speculated that the market for wooden-carved toys would remain as strong as it had been in the past, and he had bet a lot of money on that prediction—money he did not have. All he had risked initially was $3,500, but if he was wrong about the demand for the toys, he stood to lose as much as $70,000.

Along came Harvey. He was the biggest speculator of all. He was willing to predict that the toys would not only sell well but also that they would bring even higher prices than they had previously. Perhaps he knew something that Jack didn't. Maybe he was relying on the resources of his company to advertise for the toys heavily and thus raise the chances of successfully selling them. Maybe he just had a gut feeling about the toys. No matter. Whatever his reason, he was willing to pay Jack $14,000 on the possibility that hand-carved wooden cars and soldiers would sell very well even at a high price.

Jack transferred his risk to Harvey, and in so doing he locked in a fair profit for himself—not the profit he envisioned when he first made the deal with Woody, but enough to compensate him for escaping the risk of huge losses. Harvey stood to make a lot of money on the deal if his predictions were correct, but in the end he was left with all the risk if he was wrong.

## WHAT IS A FUTURES CONTRACT?

A *futures contract* is simply an agreement for a seller to deliver a specified quantity of a particular grade of a certain commodity to a predetermined location on a certain date. That's simple enough. A rancher could sign an agreement with a meat packer to deliver 44,000 pounds of 600-to-800-pound steers, 60% to 80% choice, to the packing house on a date six months hence. This would constitute a futures contract, or a contract for future delivery, just like the contract between Woody and Jack.

Neither of these contracts, however, is a futures contract capable of being traded at a commodity futures exchange. Each is a unique contract with specifications unique to that transaction. Only a few individuals would have an interest in becoming a party to either contract. Who, other than Harvey, for example, would want to speculate on wooden toys? What each of these contracts lacks is *standardization.* To be traded on the floor of a commodity futures exchange, a contract must be standardized so that the only negotiable part of the contract is price.

A typical futures contract—one that is traded presently at the Chicago Mercantile Exchange—is the contract for frozen pork bellies (slabs of bacon). This contract calls for 40,000 pounds of green, square-cut, clear, seedless bellies with 75 or fewer minor defects, cut from barrows, gilts, and smoother sows (no stags or boars permitted), to be delivered from a federally inspected packing plant in Chicago during the months of February, March, May, July, or August (the trader chooses the delivery month). Anyone who trades in pork bellies at the Chicago Mercantile Exchange will trade that particular contract. Only the price per pound will be negotiated on the trading floor.

There are many contracts negotiated every day, like that between Woody and Jack, that could be called futures contracts. The only characteristic they share, however, is that they all have a *future element*—that is, they call for future delivery of a commodity. Therefore, because the commodity is different from contract to contract, or the quantity or the delivery point or the quality varies, each contract has a very limited appeal to speculators who might otherwise be interested in buying such a contract on the assumption that conditions in the future might change the value of the commodity.

In the case of Harvey, once he bought the contract from Jack, he was virtually stuck with having to take delivery of the toys because the chances of finding someone else interested in speculating on the price of wooden toys was next to nil. In the futures industry, we call that a lack of *liquidity.*

What separates a futures contract at a futures exchange from a contract for future delivery then is the element of standardization. All commodity futures contracts traded on the trading floor of a commodity futures exchange are standardized according to quantity, grade, delivery month, and delivery point, just like the contract for pork bellies at the Chicago Mercantile Exchange.

*Transfer of Risk*

Contrary to the perception of many who are only marginally familiar with futures trading, standardized futures contracts were not established simply because a group of speculators was eager to take a chance on making a killing and needed a vehicle for that purpose. Certainly, the popular misperception of the modern commodities trader, romanticized to near-mythical status as a self-made person of great wealth—the wearer of a Rolex watch, the driver of a BMW or a Mercedes-Benz—perpetuates the mistaken impression that speculation is the sole purpose for trading futures contracts and that no legitimate economic or social benefit accrues from the buying and selling of commodity futures. Nothing could be further from the truth. The fact is that standardized commodity futures contracts were established in response to the economic risk inherent in dealing with certain perishable and/or seasonal commodities.

Ask any farmer about the risks involved in growing a crop of corn. If the weather during the growing season is ideal, the farmer will likely have a bumper crop. But so will many other farmers. Consequently, corn will flood the market, supply may exceed demand, and prices will fall. If, on the other hand, the weather during the growing season is too dry or too wet or too windy, the farmer may have a poor crop. But so will other farmers. Consequently, there won't be enough corn to meet the demand and prices will go up.

How can a farmer predict the price he will get for his corn at harvest time? The answer is, he can't, and so the very act of planting his corn becomes speculative. But most farmers don't enjoy being speculators. They want to know they will get a fair price for their product, enough to make a fair profit to provide support for their family. If they could transfer some of the risk involved in their business, they would be only too happy to do so in exchange for a degree of security.

Ask a contractor about the risk involved in building a house. When he bids a price for the home, he knows the price of lumber at that moment. He can only speculate, however, on the price he will have to pay for lumber when it comes time to purchase the materials for constructing the house. He would be very happy if he could accurately predict that price. Although not as volatile as the farmer's risk, there is, nevertheless, a risk factor.

Thus, for both producers and end users of many commodities, risk and speculation are an inherent and inescapable part of doing business. Consequently, the higher the risk that must be assumed by either, the higher the price of the product will be to the consumer to cover that risk.

The standardized futures contract provides a vehicle whereby business risk can be transferred from producers and users of commodities to speculators who are willing to take a chance in exchange for the possibility of huge profits. As the producers and users are able to transfer their risks, like Woody Carver, they are able to plan more efficiently and thus reduce the cost of doing business. The ultimate beneficiary of the futures exchange, therefore, is the consumer, who pays lower prices for the commodity.

## Price Risk

Price risk occurs as a result of time intervention in a transaction. In a complex international market, the time between production and end use of a product can often be very long, ranging from months to years. During that intervening time lag, the price of the commodity is very vulnerable to change. If the producer holds the commodity during the interval, prices could drop precipitously in the interim, creating a huge loss of income. On the other hand, prices could rise significantly, creating an additional expense for the buyer. Either way, one party to the transaction stands a chance to lose a significant amount of money while the other stands to gain unexpected profits, all because of circumstances that neither has control over.

Time alone, of course, does not create the risk. In an international market, conditions can transpire anywhere in the world that directly affect the price of a commodity: drought, flood, war, political upheaval, storms—the list could go on. An individual or a company holding large amounts of that commodity can suddenly find that the value of their stores has decreased (or increased) by substantial amounts, almost overnight. Thus, a grain buyer who may have purchased 500,000 bushels of corn from Midwest producers, utilizing credit to finance up to 90% of the transaction, could find himself in serious financial difficulty if the price were to drop 20 cents per bushel before he resells the corn to a mill.

In a complex international market, furthermore, there is often intense competition, which can bid a price up or down very quickly, resulting in broad price swings in a relatively short period of time. Other risk factors, related to supply and demand, are seasonal harvests and seasonal demand for some products.

Ultimately, the factor of time combined with unpredictable circumstances related to supply and demand creates potential price risk that is untenable to a buyer or a seller of a commodity. Some means to reduce risk is essential to the orderly transaction of business in any market subject to such volatile price changes. The standardized commodity futures contract is the instrument whereby risk can be transferred.

## THE FORWARD CONTRACT: PREDECESSOR TO THE FUTURES CONTRACT

### The History of the Futures Contract in the United States

During the 19th century, the industrial growth of the United States resulted in the steady increase of production capabilities for the farmer and a greater degree of specialization in the marketplace. Local self-sufficiency gave way to regional and national markets. The time between the production of a crop and its end use became greater. No longer could the farmer simply take a wagon load of corn to the local miller, have it ground into meal and bagged for use during the coming months, and leave some for the miller in payment for the processing. Rather, small local millers gave way to larger regional mills; small local farmers gave way to larger enterprises. Middlemen established grain elevators, where the farmer's produce could be purchased and stored for transportation to larger regional distribution and storage centers.

As the country's population moved westward, new markets opened up for industrial products, resulting in further expansion of production facilities. For the farmer, the market progressed from local to regional to national, and then to international, as production capacity grew and transportation and communication systems expanded and improved.

Chicago became a booming center of transportation and commerce, with most of the agricultural and industrial products that were headed for larger markets passing through the city. Midwest farmers in the 1830s and 1840s, however, experienced difficult problems with marketing their grains. At that time, railroads, which would later facilitate the movement of large quantities of grain to many far-flung markets, were not yet built. There were few storage facilities, which made it impossible to store the grain for future sale. As a consequence, at harvest time, farmers arriving in Chicago with their crops often created a great oversupply of grain.

This flood of grain caused prices to drop and resulted in very little return to the farmer: He was forced to accept whatever price he could get for the grain. It also caused vast spoilage, as the market could not absorb the supply of grain being brought in. Immense quantities of spoiled grain were often dumped in Lake Michigan.

A few enterprising farmers, however, began to avoid the rush to market by arranging for a future sale of their crop. They would contract with a buyer for an agreed price upon delivery of the grain at the market, perhaps two weeks hence. Later, these "to-arrive," or "forward," contracts were extended to longer periods, say, 30 to 60 days hence. Such a contract effectively transferred a degree of price risk from the farmer to the buyer. It also tended to smooth out the process of alternating gluts and shortages during the year.

With forward contracts, buyers could schedule grain deliveries at more convenient intervals. Grain elevators were able to plan the utilization of storage space more effectively. Processors could expect a steadier supply of grain without the extreme price swings that would result from the earlier oversupply/undersupply situation. Forward contracts seemed to be the perfect solution to the extreme problems of the 1830s and 1840s.

Nevertheless, some problems remained. It was not difficult, for example, for a farmer to welch on the deal if he was able to get a better price at the time of delivery. Likewise, a buyer might try to renegotiate the deal if prices had dropped in the interim.

Speculators entered the market along with the development of forward contracts. These were individuals not in the grain trade who would enter a contract in anticipation of a price change by the time of delivery. If a speculator contracted to buy a load of grain, he naturally expected that the price on the cash market at the time designated for delivery would be higher, so he could immediately sell the grain at a profit. Likewise, a speculator might agree to sell a load of grain, expecting that when the contract came due, he could buy grain at a lower price and sell at the contracted price. By so doing, some of the risk that would have been transferred to the buyer from the farmer was now transferred to the speculator. It was not uncommon for a forward contract to change hands several times before delivery actually took place.

In the absence of a regulated market, however, transacting business via forward contracts remained a difficult and risky endeavor. A buyer might hold a contract for delivery of corn at an established price, for example, but because there was no standard for quality, he was never sure exactly what was being bought until delivery took place. It was very possible that the corn being delivered would be of inferior quality. Furthermore, there was no way for a buyer or a seller to be sure the negotiated price of the forward contract was fair because prices were often kept secret. For the speculator who traded forward contracts, each transaction was a unique business deal because the size of the contracts varied as did the terms of payment and delivery. All of these shortcomings led to a loose association of grain merchants in Chicago who attempted to standardize contracts and provide some organization to the chaos of the Chicago grain market.

In 1848 the Chicago Board of Trade was established as a place where grain merchants could meet and attempt to solve some of the problems they encountered. By 1865 the Chicago Board of Trade had established standards for contract size, quality, and delivery, as well as a set of rules for trading contracts. This date marks the beginning of futures trading in the United States. The "to-arrive" contract had become a commodity futures contract.

## The Early History of the Futures Contract in Europe and Japan

In medieval Europe most business was transacted at regional market fairs, often by barter. These fairs turn up quite often in the nursery rhymes, stories, and songs we heard as children. The fair is where Jack traded the family cow for a bunch of magic beans, where Simple Simon met the pieman, and where Johnny, who stayed so long at the fair, was to have bought a bunch of blue ribbons for his love, so she could tie up her bonny brown hair.

To facilitate the orderly and honest transaction of business, the market fairs through the years became more specialized and organized, with rules that the merchants were expected to follow. If Jack had dealt with more scrupulous merchants who followed the fair regulations, he never would have incurred his mother's intense wrath. But then, neither would he have discovered the goose with the golden eggs, and we would have been denied the wonderful fantasy of the magic beanstalk.

But unlike Jack's swindling traders, most medieval merchants found that adhering to the regulations established by the fairs reduced the risk of doing business, and so they were quite willing to follow the rules. At the fairs, for example, commodities were traded at scheduled times and places, so that buyers and sellers could find each other more easily.

All traders were confined to the fairgrounds, so that side deals could not be made apart from the open market, where bids and offers were required to be public. Under such conditions, it was much more difficult for unscrupulous buyers or sellers to cheat one another or to corner the market on a particular commodity.

As open market fairs grew, there developed a sort of currency called a fair letter, which established a future cash settlement date for a transaction. With these fair letters, merchants could travel from fair to fair, using the letters as a medium of exchange in the transaction of business. These fair letters were the crude forerunners of the modern futures contract and, like the futures contract, were born out of legitimate business demands.

The first recorded example of actual futures trading occurred in Japan in 1697. Whereas the European fairs had developed the structure and rules presaging a modern futures market, they were, nevertheless, cash markets. No attempt was made to take the next step and develop an actual futures contract. Evidently, the market fairs did not present a set of circumstances that made the trading of futures contracts beneficial.

In Japan, however, the feudal system did just that. Japanese landowners found that they could use certificates of receipt against their rice crops as a sort of currency. As these certificates found their way into the economy, various individuals discovered that the value of the certificates could rise or fall as the price of rice fluctuated. Thus was born the Dojima Rice Market—the world's first futures market—where speculators traded the certificates of receipt, which were actually contracts for the future delivery of rice.

The practice of transacting these certificates of receipt, however, was little more than gambling because there was no allowance for physical delivery of the rice. When no delivery can take place, then a futures contract has little relationship to the underlying cash value of the commodity, and its value on an open exchange can fluctuate wildly and unpredictably. As a consequence, the Japanese government prohibited futures trading for a while in the 17th century. Later, with increased regulation that made physical delivery possible, the government allowed futures trading exchanges to reopen.

## THE TRADING OF THE FUTURES CONTRACT

At this time, you should have a good idea of what a futures contract is and how it has evolved historically. You now know that the reason futures contracts are traded is to transfer risk from producers and users of a commodity to speculators who hope to reap great profits. What you have yet to learn is how that transfer of risk takes place.

As said previously, a futures contract is standardized by quantity, quality, delivery date, and delivery point. This is done to encourage liquidity, which means simply a lot of traders exchanging a lot of contracts of that commodity. But by now, these thoughts have probably crossed your mind: "If I choose to enter a contract as a buyer or a seller, what happens if the contract expires and I have to make good? Where will I find all those pork bellies to deliver? What if I'm a buyer; will my freezer hold 40,000 pounds of frozen bacon?"

The fact is, you have nothing to worry about. Less than 5% of all futures transactions result in delivery. As a trader, you simply make sure that you liquidate your position prior to the delivery date of the contract.

Perhaps, though, another question has occurred to you: "What happens if a seller of livestock futures chooses to make delivery and there are no cattle around of the grade specified in the contract?" If that happens, then a different grade is delivered and a premium is charged or subtracted depending on whether the cattle to be delivered are superior to or inferior to the grade specified by the contract. Likewise, if delivery is to a different location, the cost of transporting the cattle from the contract delivery point to the requested delivery point is added to the settlement cost. However, remember, less than 5% of all futures contracts result in delivery. The vast majority of contracts are offset, or liquidated, prior to delivery.

So how do speculators make money on futures contracts if no delivery ever takes place? A commodity futures trader enters into a futures contract by agreeing to sell a commodity or buy a commodity according to the precise contract specifications established by the exchange. By entering into the contract, the speculator has also agreed to a specified price. For example, if I choose to trade a contract of corn, I may agree to sell 5,000 bushels of corn at $2.11 per bushel to be delivered in July of the current year. The position I have established is a "short" position. I could now say that I am a "short seller" or that I am "short" one contract of corn. The linguistic root of this expression is the same as if I were to say I am short of money to buy a pair of shoes. With the shoes, short means I do not have all of the money. Short in the commodities market means I will be a seller and thus be short of the commodity if delivery is taken.

Now that I have a short position in corn, I have two alternatives. One is to hold the position until the contract expires. At that time, I can arrange to buy 5,000 bushels of corn for cash and then deliver them to the buyer of my contract. If I buy the corn at less than $2.11 per bushel on the cash market, I will make money when I sell it for $2.11 per bushel to the contract buyer. On the other hand, if I have to pay more than $2.11 on the cash market, I will lose money. For example, if I pay $2.15 per bushel, I lose $0.04 per bushel times 5,000 bushels, or $200.

The other alternative available to me as a short seller is to offset, or liquidate, my position, hopefully when the futures price of corn will allow me to make a profit. I can liquidate by taking the opposite position. Since I am a seller (short), I can liquidate by becoming a buyer (going long). If this is confusing, just remember what happened when I chose to hold my position until expiration. I offset my short position by buying corn on the cash market, which I then delivered to the buyer of my contract. The same occurs here. If I have a long position and a short position, they cancel each other out, and I am out of the market.

Did I make money? If I went short at $2.11 per bushel and then went long, or liquidated, at $2.05 per bushel, I made $0.06 per bushel times 5,000 bushels, which equals $300. Don't get confused: If I buy at $2.05 and sell at $2.11, I make a profit of $0.06, regardless of the order in which I do it. The rule is always "buy low—

sell high," but it can be reversed to "sell high—buy low."

### Margin

When I decide to sell a contract of corn on the futures exchange, I don't actually sell the corn. I only agree to sell the corn at a later date. It would be the same if I were to sell my house. Usually, when a house is sold, the seller signs a sales contract agreeing to deliver title to the house at a closing, which normally occurs 60 to 90 days later. When the title is delivered, payment is made from the buyer to the seller. In the meantime, the buyer puts up earnest money to indicate he intends to honor the contract and actually buy the house when the closing date arrives. Remember the $3,500 that Jack deposited as earnest money with Woody when they signed their contract. Although the actual transaction would take place later, the deposit indicated Jack's intention to follow through on the deal.

Likewise, a futures contract is only an agreement that a transaction will take place later. Consequently, no money changes hands until the transaction occurs at its scheduled date. Each party to the transaction, however, must put up earnest money to guarantee that they will live up to the terms of the contract. In the case of the house, only the buyer puts up earnest money. In the futures market, both parties to the transaction put up earnest money, which is called *margin*. Margin usually amounts to approximately 5% to 10% of the contract value. This is called *initial margin*.

If a trade moves against me, that is, prices change so that I am losing money on my position, I might have to put up additional money, as my initial margin is being used to cover my losses. The futures exchange requires that I maintain a certain amount of margin in my account. This is called *maintenance margin*. Thus, it may be that I have to put up $2,000 in initial margin money to make a trade, with the understanding that I will maintain at least $1,500 in margin if the trade moves against me.

*Hedging*

Now we know how a speculator makes or loses money in the futures market. Earlier we said that the primary function of the futures exchange is to transfer risk to the speculator. This occurs through a process known as *hedging.* Heding occurs when a producer or user takes a position in the futures market that is the same as his position in the cash market.

Thus, if a farmer is raising cattle and he intends to bring them to market in six months, he can hedge his risk by taking a futures position in cattle, which is the same as his intended cash transaction. Since he intends to sell cattle for cash in six months, he can sell a futures contract for cattle now. If the price of cattle goes up in six months, the farmer will make more money on his cattle but will lose money on the futures position (he will have bought high and sold low). Conversely, if the price of cattle declines, the farmer will lose money in the cash market will make money in the futures market. By hedging, the farmer has cut his profit potential as well as his risk of loss. His cash position and his futures position balance one another, and his price six months hence is locked in.

CHAPTER 3

# The Modern Futures Exchange

In Chicago, there is a three-block stretch of LaSalle Street known as The Canyon. As you walk south along these three blocks, you understand the reason for this popularized appellation. Lining the street on both sides are dark, imposing stone, concrete, and brick buildings, which block the sun from the street during most of the day. Even on relatively warm days, cold, sharp winds rush through The Canyon and threaten the unwary pedestrian.

The buildings along this section of LaSalle Street were built to house the great financial institutions of the Midwest. Here you find Continental Illinois Bank, the beneficiary of a massive Federal bail out in 1983, after unwary bank officials invested too many assets in the Oklahoma oil boom through their relationship with the previously little-known but, after the debacle, infamous Penn Square Bank.

Across the street from Continental Illinois Bank is the Federal Reserve Bank of Chicago. Up and down LaSalle Street are many of the 80 or so foreign bank branches and representative offices to which Chicago is home. Here, too, you can see the Harris Bank, the American National Bank, the Exchange National Bank, and the list goes on.

Not as well known in public lore as Wall Street, LaSalle Street is nevertheless a very imposing and quite proper center of international banking and finance. Chicago locals know that when you are on the Lake Michigan shore just north of downtown, you are on the Gold Coast, but when you are here on LaSalle Street in The Canyon, you are near the gold.

As with many canyon formations that occur naturally in mountainous terrain, the LaSalle Street Canyon, here on the plains of Illinois, near the shore of Lake Michigan, is a box canyon. At the southern end of this man-made gorge, blocking any further advance of LaSalle Street, as well as most of the sunlight from the canyon, is a tall, narrow, dark-stained stone edifice, looking very much like an obelisk or a mystical monument. The top of this huge tower is scaled back, forming a sort of pyramid, at whose apex, far above street level, stands an imposing goddess of fertility, looking out on the infertile concrete, brick, and stone of this great city that is spread beneath her. This is the Chicago Board of Trade (CBOT).

Stretching vertically along the north face of the CBOT building are narrow five-storey-high windows, behind which is one of the two huge trading floors of the CBOT. Ironically, these windows served an important function when the CBOT first moved into this building in 1928. At that time, the CBOT was primarily a grain exchange, and sample bags of the various grades of grain were kept around the floor. The windows allowed traders plenty of natural light by which to inspect the various bags of grains. Today, these majestic windows are mostly hidden to the traders on the floor by long blackout shades, and the activity in this north trading floor has been entirely given over to the trading of various financial and interest rate futures rather than grains. Here in the Bond Room of the CBOT, traders deal in U.S. Treasury Bond futures and options, municipal bond futures and options, and other similar financial instruments, none of which would have been recognized, or even thought of, as a legitimate member of the commodity futures industry back in 1928.

Today's CBOT is the world's largest and oldest futures exchange, accounting for nearly half the volume of all the futures trading done in the United States. However, with the proliferation of new contracts being added each year and with the growing popularity of financial futures and stock indices eclipsing the more traditional contracts in grains and livestock, the CBOT finds itself being challenged from around the world for the position of being the largest. In fact, just down the street and over a few blocks stand the recently constructed twin towers of the Chicago Mercantile Exchange building with the two red-stone office towers connected by the ultramodern trading floors of the Chicago Mercantile Exchange (CME). With over 70,000 square feet of trading area, the CME consistently challenges the CBOT by gaining an ever-increasing share of the futures business. The two exchanges together account for 10 of the futures industry's 12 most actively traded futures contracts.

In addition to the CBOT and the CME, there are nine other major futures exchanges in the United States. Of the 11 exchanges, five are in New York: (1) The Coffee, Sugar and Cocoa Exchange, (2) The Commodity Exchange, Inc. (COMEX), (3) The New York Cotton Exchange, (4) The New York Futures Exchange (NYFE), and (5) The New York Mercantile Exchange. Three exchanges are in Chicago: (1) The Chicago Board of Trade (CBOT), (2) The Chicago Mercantile Exchange (CME), and (3) The Mid-America Commodity Exchange (MidAm). Of the three other exchanges, one is in Kansas City (The Kansas City Board of Trade), one in Minneapolis (The Minneapolis Grain Exchange), and one in Philadelphia (The Philadelphia Board of Trade).

Internationally, the number of exchanges has been growing faster than in the United States, as major economic centers have rushed to service the ever-increasing demand for new instruments to hedge against fluctuating interest rates, ever-changing foreign exchange rates, and institutional securities portfolios. There are presently 23 foreign futures exchanges, located in Toronto, Winnipeg, London, Sao Paulo, Rio de Janeiro, Sydney, Amsterdam, Hong Kong, Bermuda, Kuala Lumpur, Paris, Auckland, Osaka, Singapore, Stockholm, Zurich, and Tokyo.

## *THE PURPOSE OF THE FUTURES EXCHANGE*

The modern futures exchange exists for the purpose of bringing buyers and sellers together and providing a facility where futures trading can take place. In most exchanges, this means a trading floor where buyers and sellers physically meet in an area known as the trading pit. In four of the foreign exchanges, specifically the New Zealand Futures Exchange, The Stockholm Options Market, The Swiss Options and Financial Futures Exchange, and the Bermuda Exchange, the trading facility is a computerized, fully automated program for electronic trading from remote computer screens. Although some of the major domestic exchanges have also established some electronically traded contracts, most futures trading still occurs by open outcry auction on the trading floor of the exchange.

So that business will be transacted in an efficient, fair, and ethical manner, the exchange supervises all trading that is conducted on the trading floor and establishes the rules by which trading is to occur. In addition, the exchange collects and disseminates the price and volume information so that speculators off the floor will know what the market is.

In order to facilitate the orderly and honest transaction of business, the modern futures exchange is highly organized and operates under a strict set of rules and regulations. Most exchanges are nonprofit organizations, where members serving on various committees and boards regulate and oversee the operation of the exchange and its paid administrative staff. Members of the exchange, who have paid the current asking price for their membership, or "seat," also enjoy the privilege of access to the trading floor, where they may operate as a floor trader if they choose. Table 3-1 depicts a typical organizational chart of the modern futures exchange.

## MANAGEMENT AND ORGANIZATION OF THE EXCHANGE

The daily affairs of the futures exchange are managed by a chief executive officer, usually known as the president. This is a salaried position appointed by the

TABLE 3-1. BOARD OF GOVERNORS (MEMBERS AND NONMEMBERS).

| Clearing Members | President (Salaried) | Committees (Members) |
|---|---|---|
| Members | Staff (paid) | Staff (paid) |
| | Research | Clearinghouse |
| | Education | Floor Practices |
| | Audits and | Business Conduct |
| | Investigations | |
| | Quotations | Contact |
| | | Specifications |
| | Statistical | Rules |
| | Public Relations | Pit |
| | | Floor Brokers |
| | | Membership |
| | | Public Relations |
| | | Arbitration |

Board of Governors, who govern the exchange by establishing major policies and setting the rules by which the exchange will operate. The Board of Governors is usually comprised of both members and nonmembers, and it is elected by the exchange membership. Nonmembers on the Board of Governors represent both the general public and businesses that have an interest in futures trading.

One of the tasks of the Board of Governors is to establish the number of memberships in the exchange. All memberships are privately held, and a change in membership occurs through a bid-and-offer process. Thus, the price of a seat on the exchange will fluctuate depending on demand.

A prospective member applying for a seat on the exchange must pass muster with the exchange members by submitting to a thorough investigation of his or her financial background and personal character. After passing the investigation, the applicant is presented to the Board of Governors for approval. Once approved, the new member may exercise the four privileges of exchange membership:

* *Access to the trading floor.*

* *The right to function as a floor trader.*

* *Reduced commissions on trades.*

* *Participation in the management of the exchange.*

Members become involved in the management of the exchange by serving on one of several committees:

* The Clearinghouse Committee determines the required qualifications to be a clearing member and passes judgment on applicants.

* The Floor Practice Committee oversees all floor activity and deals with issues of trading ethics and price discrepancies.

* The Business Conduct Committee maintains orderly and businesslike trading practices by assuring the integrity of the members.

* The Contract Specifications Committee reviews existing contracts and recommends changes to the Board of Governors.

* The Rules Committee reviews existing rules and recommends rule changes or new rules to the Board of Governors.

* The Pit Committee assures the orderly opening and closing of trading and operates as arbiter regarding price discrepancies that occur during trading.

* The Floor Brokers Committee assures the qualifications of all brokers and floor traders.

* The Membership Committee reviews the financial background and personal character of all prospective members.

* The Public Relations Committee oversees matters pertaining to publicity and public relations.

* The Arbitration Committee resolves disputes between members.

The day-to-day activities of the exchange are carried out by the exchange staff under the direction of the president. The staff is usually organized into departments of which the following are typical:

* The Audit and Investigations Department monitors members' firms for financial strength and ethical practices and collects information on prospective members of the exchange and the clearinghouse.

* The Statistical Department disseminates daily price data.

* The Quotations Department oversees the posting of price data on the trading floor and over the wire services.

* The Research Department researches new contracts and possible changes in existing contracts.

* The Education Department provides information to hedgers, speculators, brokers, and the public.

* The Public Relations Department manages publicity for the exchange.

### The Clearinghouse

One of the most important divisions of the futures exchange is the *clearinghouse,* which is an adjunct to the exchange. All clearing members are members of the exchange, but not every exchange member is a member of the clearinghouse; some clearinghouses are integral divisions of the exchange whereas others are separate corporate entities. All clearinghouses provide essentially the same functions for the exchange, though. One of those functions is to facilitate the exchange of funds as member firms transact business.

Another important clearinghouse operation is to settle all transactions that are executed on the trading floor by matching all purchases and sales. Through a process called *tradechecking,* all transactions are settled daily. The clearinghouse then takes the opposite side of all the contracts traded that day, thereby guaranteeing the contractual obligations of each transaction.

The financial integrity of the futures exchange rests on the solvency of the clearing members. Therefore, exchanges establish minimum capital requirements for clearing members, requiring that they maintain as much as several million dollars on deposit with the clearinghouse, the amount depending on the number of contracts being guaranteed by the clearing members.

The futures exchange closely monitors the financial activities and condition of each clearing member through regular financial reporting, surveillance, on-site audits, and sharing of financial information with other exchanges. The exchange may, in an emergency, call for immediate capital increases in margins on deposit, re- ductions in positions, or early settlement, thus allowing the exchange to take immediate action on the basis of financial information it may obtain regarding a clearing member firm.

Any exchange member wishing to trade on the ex- change must either be a clearing member or have a relationship with a clearing member. All trades must be registered with and settled through that clearing member.

### Clearing Trades

The most important function of the clearinghouse is to "clear" all trades. That is, the clearinghouse takes the opposite side of all trades. At the end of each trading day, all transactions between floor brokers are confirmed. At that time, all confirmed trades are tallied by the clearing member to whom the broker is responsible, then checked by the clearinghouse. After all trades have been matched, the clearinghouse becomes the seller to all buyers, and the buyer to all sellers. Thus, the trade is cleared, and the traders no longer have an obligation to the opposite party in the original transaction.

This activity of clearing trades serves three essential functions of the exchange. First, the liquidity of the market is maintained because all positions can be offset by the trader simply taking the opposite position later. That is, if a trader is long in soybeans because he bought one contract, the opposite party to his contract is the clearinghouse. Therefore, if the trader wishes to liquidate his position (get out of his obligation), he simply must sell a contract to the exchange. This offsetting position relieves the trader of any further contractual responsi- bility, and he did not have to look up the original trading partner to do it.

Second, if delivery of the contract is to take place (only 5% or fewer of all futures contracts result in de- livery), the process is much easier when the clearing- house is the opposite party. The trader wishing to make delivery simply notifies the clearinghouse, which then notifies the trader with the oldest existing long position (contract to buy) that delivery is to take place. None of the traders who may have handled one side or the other of that contract during its life needs to be involved in the delivery transaction in any way.

Third, if one party to a contract defaults for any reason, the fulfillment of the contract is guaranteed by the clearinghouse, which is now the opposite party to the transaction. All clearing members contribute to a special fund to be used to fulfill contractual or financial obligations of members who default.

## THE ROLE OF THE EXCHANGE IN FUTURES TRADING

We have said that there are important sectors in an open market economy where risk is the result of either a time factor (delivery is to take place much later, when prices have declined) or a distance factor (delivery must take place a long distance away, where prices might be significantly lower or the currency might be different and adversely affect price). We have said that futures contracts allow the legitimate producer or user (hedger) to transfer that risk to a speculator who is willing to assume the risk because of the possibility of great profitability if prices move the right way. The role of the exchange, we have said, is to bring together the buyers and the sellers, the hedgers and the speculators in an orderly, efficient manner. In the process of bringing together the players in a futures transaction, the exchange performs four vital roles for the open market economy: price discovery, risk transfer, liquidity, and standardization.

### Price Discovery

As sellers offer to sell and buyers offer to buy in the pit, they provide immediate information regarding the price of the futures contract. The price is usually given as a "bid-ask." For example, the price for corn might be $2.40 bid, $2.42 ask, meaning a buyer is willing to pay $2.40 a bushel, but the seller wants $2.42 a bushel.

### Risk Transfer

In a futures transaction, risk is not created as it is in a gambling situation. A gambler creates risk by choosing to bet money on the roll of the dice or the turn of a card. If he chooses not to gamble, there is no risk. In a futures transaction, as we have seen, the risk is an inherent part of doing business. The exchange provides a setting where risk can be transferred from the hedgers to the speculators.

### Liquidity

If risk is to be transferred efficiently, there must be a large group of individuals ready to buy or sell. When a hedger wants to sell futures contracts to protect his business position, he can't afford to wait around for a long time for a buyer. He needs to know he can effect the transaction quickly. The futures exchange brings together a large number of speculators, thus making quick transactions possible. Moreover, by clearing all trades, the exchange allows contracts to be bought and sold rapidly.

### Standardization

The exchange writes the specifications for each contract, setting standards of grading, measurement, methods of transfer, and times of delivery. By standardizing the contracts in this manner, the exchange opens the futures market up to almost anyone willing to hedge risk. In the pits, then, the auction process is facilitated because only price must be negotiated.

It is important to remember that the exchange does not own or trade contracts. It simply provides a market

where that can occur. The exchange does not set prices—
the activity on the trading floor, in the pits where price
is discovered through open outcry auction, establishes
prices. The exchange does disseminate price information
so that speculators and hedgers not on the trading floor
may know what the market is.


## ELEMENTS OF FUTURES TRADING AT THE FUTURES EXCHANGE

Remember that any kind of contract trading can
include a futures element. If you're buying a car, you
can arrange for future delivery at a specified date, at an
agreed-upon location and price, with options you chose,
in a color you selected. If you are a commercial buyer,
you can order a quantity of merchandise for futures
delivery at an established price. Futures trading, as we
have seen, is something more than simply contracting
for a future consummation of a business transaction.

Futures trading, as it is done through an organized
futures exchange, involves several specific elements:

1. All trading is done in a specified area according
to an established set of rules. This area is known as the
pit.

2. All trading is done within specified hours. No
trading may occur outside these scheduled trading times,
although different commodities will have different trading
hours.

3. All trading is done by open outcry. Therefore, all
bids and offers are known to all participants, and all
transactions are public knowledge. No orders may be
filled without open outcry.

4. All trading is done in contracts that are standardized for quality (grade), delivery date, location, procedure, and contract size.

5. Negotiation in the pit is limited to price only (bid-ask).

6. If a contract is to be fulfilled by arranging delivery (which occurs in less than 10% of the trades), a premium or discount will be attached to the price for any differential from the contract specifications.

7. The exchange clearinghouse assumes the opposite side of all trades. The buyer and seller negotiate price, after which each has an obligation with the clearinghouse, not with each other. This is important when the positions are later liquidated, as it would be very difficult to find the original buyer or seller, who might not be of a mind to cancel the contract at that time or price, anyway.

8. All futures contracts can legally be canceled by taking an offsetting position. Therefore, if a trader buys six contracts of December corn, and later sells six contracts of December corn, the original position is deemed liquidated, and there is no more obligation to either contract.

9. The exchange clearinghouse guarantees all contracts. To do this, the clearinghouse requires that a member's account have a minimum amount of capital in it (specified by the exchange), from which a preestablished margin amount is obligated as earnest money when a futures contract is entered into.

# CHAPTER 4

# The Variety of Futures Markets

The futures trading industry originally developed in the United States out of a need to transfer risk from the everyday business of buying and selling grain in Chicago. Today, at the Chicago Board of Trade, grain futures are still traded much as they have been for over 100 years. The soybean and its derivatives, soybean oil and meal, have joined the traditional grains—corn, oats, and wheat—as popular and heavily traded futures contracts at the CBOT. Although grain futures are still a significant part of the futures industry, the business of trading futures contracts has grown far beyond the grain markets in scope and popularity.

Historically, wherever a high degree of price risk is attached to doing business because of the effect of time or distance on price, futures trading has been likely to develop. In the 1840s, price risk primarily occurred in the grain markets of Chicago, and the Chicago Board of Trade responded in 1865 with the organized trading of futures contacts. (Even though the CBOT was established in 1848, a formal set of rules for trading futures contracts was not written until 1865, which is a more accurate date from which to mark the beginning of futures trading in the United States.) But at this same time, other agricultural markets were also flourishing in Chicago, which in the 1850s and 1860s had become the nucleus of the nation's agricultural marketing system. The convergence of canals, rivers, lakes, and railroads made Chicago the center of transportation for the country and the distribution point for a wide variety of agricultural products.

The great cattle drives, which have been romanticized in books and motion pictures, often ended in the legendary Chicago stockyards during this period, as the railroads brought carload after carload of cattle into the city to be sold to the meatpackers—the Armours, the Cudahys, the Swifts, and the lesser-known packing houses. The recently refurbished Chicago Amphitheatre, where stock sales, rodeos, and presidential conventions have often been held, still stands as testament to the activity of that lively era. However, the historic Stockyard Inn, which was often host to presidents and cowboys alike, was demolished just a few years ago.

The area where the Chicago stockyards were once located, just south of downtown, is now an industrial park, although several expanses of land as well as a memorial gateway arch remain as testament to an era when cowboys roamed the streets and the smell of the yards could threaten even the strongest stomach. Vestiges of the era when Chicago was, in the words of Carl Sandburg, "meat packer to the world", are visible along Halsted Street around the old stockyard area, as many small meat-processing plants continue to do a lively business. The live cattle and hogs are gone from Chicago, however, as are the drovers and the great railroad yards.

Downtown at the Chicago Mercantile Exchange, live cattle and hog futures are still traded as are pork bellies and feeder cattle. But the great stockyards are now located near Omaha, Nebraska, where, if you drive along I-80 on a hot summer day with the wind blowing in your direction, you can experience the odors, the noise, and the confusion of activity that must have kept many a hardy Chicagoan from a good night's sleep just a few decades ago.

But grains and livestock were not the only agricultural products marketed in Chicago during the last half of the 19th century. Not far from the present location of the Chicago Mercantile Exchange in downtown Chicago, right along the Chicago River, is the site of the old South Water Street Market, the historic farmers' market in Chicago. Here, on May 20, 1874, a group of South Water Street suppliers and merchants organized the Chicago Produce Exchange to provide an efficient market for butter, eggs, poultry, and other farm products.

In 1895 a dissident group of dealers, dissatisfied with market quotations, formed a division within the exchange to "establish official quotations." In 1899 this group established a separate organization called the Chicago Butter and Egg Board, which in 1919 became the Chicago Mercantile Exchange. That year, the CME clearinghouse was established to process futures transactions, and on December 1, 1919, the first futures contracts for eggs were traded at the newly formed CME.

From then until 1945, the CME traded futures in eggs, butter, cheese, potatoes, and onions. Later, the exchange added contracts in apples, poultry, and frozen eggs, and in 1954 iron and scrap steel. None of these earlier futures contracts has endured as a viable futures market at the CME. They have been replaced with livestock futures, currency futures, interest rate futures, and stock index futures.

Every Friday morning, however, at the northeast corner of the recently constructed main trading floor of the new CME building, the exchange recalls a bit of its past, with the same nostalgia one saves for a walk through the old homestead or a quiet browse through a box of familiar snapshots. Here, away from the pits and the frenetic activity of the trading floor, a clerk sets up an old blackboard and, in the same manner in which trading was conducted for decades prior to the advent of electronic quote boards, invites bids and offers on butter futures. This weekly anachronism begins at 9:30 A.M., and ends when no more bids or offers are forthcoming, usually around 10:00 A.M.

Toward the conclusion of the trading period, the clerk who is conducting the trading calls for any additional bids or offers, using the exchange public address system so that the entire trading floor can hear. Before ending the session, the clerk must call three times for any further interest in trading butter: "Any more trading in butter? Any more trading in butter? Any more trading in butter?" blares loudly over the P.A. Often, the clerk is cut off in mid-question by a bid or an offer, so that the question sounds like, "Any more trading in buh . . .?" This process may be repeated several times, as traders interrupt the call to place an order. Finally, when there are no more buyers or sellers, the three public warnings are completed, and spontaneous applause breaks out across the trading floor as the exchange of butter futures ends for another week.

The irony of this weekly exercise is that only a few yards away from the butter traders are the pits where Eurodollars, U.S. Treasury bills, and S&P 500 Stock Index futures are being traded by hundreds of wildly gesticulating and urgently yelling floor traders. The unlikely proximity of those very modern, exotic contracts to the quaint butter futures trading is testament to the rapid, extensive expansion of the futures industry during the past two decades.

It is significant that these days the successor to the Butter and Egg Board trades only a little butter (the contract is not listed by the CME) and no more eggs (fresh white eggs are listed as an inactive contract at the CME), for it reflects the direction taken by the entire industry since the early 1970s. The futures business is no longer focused primarily on agricultural commodities, and the term "futures trader" has become much more accurate than the former "commodities trader."

## A PROLIFERATION OF FUTURES MARKETS

Just as in the last half of the 19th century, when a localized economy grew into a regionalized economy, then into a national economy and finally into an international economy, the world marketplace continues to expand and to become ever more complex. The traditional commodity futures markets—grains, cotton, livestock— have been upstaged in the past 15 years by the burgeoning growth of futures trading in several related, though quite different, markets.

### Foreign Currency Futures

As international trade has grown, the relative value of one country's currency against another's has become a critical factor in the profitability of businesses in every part of the economy. The Bretton Woods agreement after World War II attempted to stabilize world currencies by establishing narrow zones within which the U.S. dollar and other currencies could fluctuate. In the early 1970s, however, this agreement began to break down, resulting in increasing volatility in international exchange rates.

This volatility increased the risk of engaging in international trade. Just as with the agricultural markets in the 1830s and 1840s, there were speculators willing to assume this risk from legitimate businessmen, who were only too happy to transfer that risk through hedging.

As a result of these actions, the futures industry, which had been largely confined to agricultural commodities for more than a century, began in the 1970s to expand into new areas. Money itself became a commodity to be traded, as foreign currencies fluctuated, often wildly, against each other and the U.S. dollar. The world financial community looked for ways to hedge against the risk of doing business in the face of unstable exchange rates, and the futures industry responded.

In 1972 the CME established the International Monetary Market (IMM) division and initiated trading in seven foreign currency futures contracts. Other futures exchanges have followed suit, and most of the world's major currencies are now being traded on the floors of futures exchanges worldwide.

But just what is a *foreign currency future?* As we saw in Chapter 2, the concept of a futures contract is, in itself, very difficult to comprehend. But as we proceeded through the development from a cash sale of a commodity to a forward, or to-arrive, contract to a futures contract, the concept became more understandable. With currency futures, however, we have no underlying commodity to function as part of the exchange. There is no corn that ultimately will be delivered for a cash payment. There is only the cash itself. How do we develop a futures contract from that?

For anyone who has traveled outside the United States, the idea of trading in currencies is rather easy to understand. As you cross the border into one country from another country—let's say, into France from Germany—you must get rid of the money from the country you are leaving (deutsche marks) and obtain currency from the country you are entering (francs). Otherwise, when you stop to buy lunch later, you may go hungry when you offer deutsche marks and the restaurant accepts only francs.

Now, if France has been experiencing an inflationary period, which results in the constantly declining value of the franc (as inflation continues, one franc will buy less of a commodity as the price of the commodity goes up), and Germany, on the other hand, has been enjoying very low inflation, the value of the deutsche mark in comparison to the franc will increase. When you cross the border into France and stop at the currency exchange, therefore, you will trade deutsche marks for francs at the current rate of exchange, which may be different at that time than the day before or the week before.

Let's say that you originally traveled from France to Germany two weeks earlier and exchanged money as you entered Germany. You bought deutsche marks using francs as currency. Now, two weeks later, you reenter France, so you wish to sell the deutsche marks still in your possession. But in the meantime, the value of the franc has dropped, and you now are able to sell your deutsche marks for more francs than you paid for them. In this situation, the deutsche mark is said to be stronger against the franc—the franc weaker against the deutsche mark. All you know is that your deutsche marks are worth more francs than when you left France two weeks ago.

In this simple example, you can readily see how currency can become a commodity to be bought and sold. For the average tourist, the fluctuation of currencies is little more than a mild irritant during the course of a vacation trip. To a merchant who imports or exports products from abroad, however, the shifting values of worldwide currencies can represent a major risk factor over which little control can be exercised.

If I am an automobile distributor, for instance, and I place an order for 20 million dollars worth of German cars to be delivered in three months, I face the risk that when I pay for the cars the value of the deutsche mark, which I must use to pay the manufacturer, may have gone up in relationship to the dollar. In other words, when I order the cars, my U.S. dollar is worth a certain number of German deutsche marks, a value we will call $x$. Three months from now, however, when I draw money from my bank in the United States to pay for the cars, the deutsche mark is worth $x + y$ dollars, $y$ representing the amount by which the deutsche mark has increased in value.

To buy the cars from the German manufacturer, I must first buy deutsche marks, just as you had to when you traveled from France into Germany, but deutsche marks cost more now. The price of the cars is the same. The price of the money to pay for the cars has gone up. I must now sell the cars for more money in the United States. If I am to preserve my profits. Alternatively, I will have to take less profit.

Of course, the opposite might also happen. The deutsche mark might drop in value, meaning I could buy more deutsche marks with my U.S. dollars three months hence. If that happens, I will make a larger profit than I had planned, or I can reduce the price of the cars in the United States. Either way, the risk involved in the transaction is more than I care to assume. I would like to find a speculator willing to relieve me of that risk. That is why futures exchanges offer contracts in foreign currency futures.

With agricultural commodity futures, the hedgers are the producers and the users: the farmers, the mills, the packinghouses. With foreign currency futures, the hedgers are the banks that must often exchange large amounts of foreign currency, corporations that must do business abroad, and foreign exchange brokers and institutional investors who invest in foreign securities.

### Interest Rate Futures

The success of foreign currency futures has led to the development of futures contracts in another area of monetary risk—fluctuating interest rates. Anyone who has purchased a house in the last 10 years is familiar with the risk associated with unstable interest rates. It is possible, and at times quite likely, for home mortgage rates to change as much as two or three percentage points in the 60 days normally required to close a real estate deal. During particularly volatile periods, a person unable to "lock in" a rate when the mortgage application is filed can sometimes end up paying a lot of extra money each month in higher interest rates.

Likewise, interest rate volatility represents a large risk to businesses and investors who count the interest earned or paid on borrowed money as a source of profit or expense. If I am a banker, for instance, I may want to invest some of my bank's assets in government securities. The amount of interest those securities earn will directly affect the profitability of my bank. Therefore, volatile interest rates represent a major financial risk to me. I don't want to speculate on what interest rates will be three, six, or 12 months from now. But there are speculators willing to assume that risk by trading *interest rate futures* contracts. Thus, I might want to hedge my government securities with an interest rate futures contract.

The most highly traded interest rate futures contract for several years has been the U.S. Treasury bond contract. Originated at the CBOT in 1977, T-bond futures are now traded in London, Singapore, and Sydney as well. The first interest rate futures contract was the (GNMA) contract at the CBOT, which began trading in 1975. At this writing, interest rate futures are trading at 15 exchanges worldwide.

### Stock Index Futures

A person responsible for the assets of a large pension fund or mutual fund who must maintain a productive, well-balanced portfolio of investments understands the risk involved in owning millions of dollars worth of stocks. After the stock market crash of October 19, 1987, that risk has become particularly apparent. In 1982 the futures industry responded to the need to hedge such risks by offering the first *stock index futures* contract, the Value Line Index, at the Kansas City Board of Trade. Five years of planning and negotiating solutions to regulatory problems preceded the inauguration of the Value

Line Index, which is based on the Value Line Average (VLA), an index of 1,700 stocks. In 1982 the Chicago Mercantile Exchange established the S&P 500 Stock Index futures and the New York Futures Exchange offered the New York Stock Exchange Index. A new era in trading futures had begun.

In its first year of existence, the S&P 500 Index became the 10th most actively traded contract in the world. By 1986 it was second only to the T-bond contract at the CBOT in total volume. At this writing, 22 different stock indexes are actively traded in exchanges worldwide with others awaiting approval.

### Cash Settlement

It is easy to visualize a trader taking delivery of a contract of pork bellies. They are a commodity that can be seen and touched. It is not difficult to imagine taking delivery of a contract of U.S. Treasury bills or even foreign currency. But how does a trader take delivery of a stock index, which has no substance and cannot be seen or touched? The answer is by *cash settlement*.

In a cash settlement, if a futures contract has come due for delivery, the two parties can settle for the difference between the price of the contract that day and the price on the day they first made the contract. Thus, a trader does not have to go out and buy a share of stock in each of the companies included in the index in order to fulfill the contract. Cash settlement of a futures contract was first implemented with the Eurodollar contract at the CME in 1981 (Eurodollars are U.S. dollars on deposit in European banks).

### Explosive Growth

The Chicago Board of Trade had a full-time staff of only 80 people in 1973. In 1987, only 14 years later, the CBOT employed over 450 full-time persons. In that same time period, the total volume of trading in futures contracts grew from just over 18 million (1972) to more than 184 million (1986), a 10-fold increase in 14 years.

Nearly overnight, it seems, the nature of futures trading has changed so as to be almost unrecognizable from the commodity futures industry prior to 1970. Table 4-1 graphically illustrates the rate at which these changes occurred.

In 1972, of the top 10 most actively traded futures contracts, eight were agricultural futures. The other two were silver contracts. In 1977, although the order had changed, and live hogs had replaced sugar, the lineup remained eight agricultural and two silver. But only five years later, in 1982, T-bonds had risen to the top of the list, only five years after its inception. In its inaugural year, the S&P 500 Index was in 10th place, after having traded less than a full year! Altogether, agricultural futures held only six of the top 10 places, and silver was no longer on the list.

Four years after that, in 1986, agricultural futures had been nearly eclipsed by financial, stock index, and currency futures. Only three agricultural contracts remained in the top 10, none among the top five. In that year, T-bonds alone traded more than twice the total number of futures contracts traded in all markets in 1972.

Today, new contracts are being developed so rapidly that it becomes difficult to keep up. Table 4-2 lists the futures contracts currently available at futures exchanges in the United States. By the time of publication of this book, the list will be outdated, as new contracts are continually being developed. Nevertheless, the list reveals the breadth of selection available to speculators and hedgers.

## A 24-HOUR WORLDWIDE MARKET

Just as new contracts are being added to futures exchanges in the United States, thus expanding the industry exponentially, so too are new contracts and new

TABLE 4-1.   CAPTION TO COME.

| | | *1972* | |
|---|---|---|---|
| 1 | Soybeans | CBT | 4,043,474 |
| 2 | Pork bellies | CME | 2,057,064 |
| 3 | Corn | CBT | 1,942,120 |
| 4 | Live cattle | CME | 1,370,471 |
| 5 | Soybean oil | CBT | 1,110,776 |
| 6 | Sugar | NYSE | 875,178 |
| 7 | Wheat | CBT | 855,813 |
| 8 | Silver | COMEX | 815,168 |
| 9 | Silver | CBT | 813,492 |
| 10 | Soybean meal | CBT | 630,916 |

Total all contracts          18,332,055

| | | *1977* | |
|---|---|---|---|
| 1 | Soybeans | CBT | 7,996,139 |
| 2 | Corn | CBT | 5,021,827 |
| 3 | Silver | COMEX | 3,573,301 |
| 4 | Live cattle | CME | 2,639,517 |
| 5 | Soybean oil | CBT | 2,535,046 |
| 6 | Soybean meal | CBT | 2,373,453 |
| 7 | Silver | CBT | 2,257,059 |
| 8 | Pork bellies | CME | 1,358,730 |
| 9 | Live hogs | CME | 1,307,712 |

Total all contracts          42,880,318

| | | *1982* | |
|---|---|---|---|
| 1 | T-bonds | CBT | 16,739,695 |
| 2 | Gold | COMEX | 12,289,448 |
| 3 | Soybeans | CBT | 9,165,520 |
| 4 | Corn | CBT | 7,948,257 |
| 5 | T-bills | CME | 6,598,848 |
| 6 | Live cattle | CME | 4,440,992 |
| 7 | Wheat | CBT | 4,031,584 |
| 8 | Live hogs | CME | 3,560,974 |
| 9 | Soybean oil | CBT | 3,049,313 |
| 10 | S&P 500 Index | CME | 2,935,532 |

Total all contracts      112,400,879

TABLE 4-1.  CAPTION TO COME *(continued)*.

|    |              |       | *1986*       |
|----|--------------|-------|--------------|
| 1  | T-bonds      | CBT   | 52,598,811   |
| 2  | S&P 500 Index| CME   | 19,505,273   |
| 3  | Eurodollar   | CME   | 10,824,914   |
| 4  | Gold         | COMEX | 8,400,175    |
| 5  | Crude oil    | NYMEX | 8,313,529    |
| 6  | Deutsche mark| CME   | 6,582,145    |
| 7  | Corn         | CBT   | 6,160,298    |
| 8  | Soybeans     | CBT   | 6,133,668    |
| 9  | Swiss franc  | CME   | 4,998,430    |
| 10 | Live cattle  | CME   | 4,690,638    |

Total contracts        184,354,496

Source:  *Futures Magazine.*

exchanges being developed around the world in various centers of commerce and finance. The futures industry is at the forefront in the development of a unified, integrated worldwide economy.

On October 19, 1987, as the Dow Jones plummeted, the news was full of disastrous plunges occurring in stock exchanges worldwide: London, Tokyo, Singapore. The panic of that day carried from one economic center to another, just like a tidal wave washing across the face of the world, knocking the foundations from under the great financial institutions of the world as it went. Would such an event have occurred 15 years ago with such velocity? Probably not. But as the news of the worldwide economic panic surrounded us all, we became acutely aware of just how thoroughly the world's marketplaces have become integrated and interdependent during the past decade.

The development of satellite communication has probably contributed more than anything else to the precipitous internationalization of the economy. As the facility for instantaneous worldwide communication has become both economically and technologically available, the world's mercantilists and speculators have rushed to utilize its full potential. As a result, exchanges around

TABLE 4-2.   U.S. FUTURES CONTRACTS.

## Chicago Board of Trade

| | | |
|---|---|---|
| Corn | GNMA CDR | Institutional Index |
| Oats | GNMA | Gold (100 troy oz.) |
| Soybeans | U.S. Treasury bond | Gold (1 kilo) |
| Soybean meal | U.S. Treasury note | Silver (5,000 troy oz.) |
| Soybean oil | Municipal Bond Index | Silver (1,000 troy oz.) |
| Wheat | Major Market Index–Maxi | |

## Chicago Mercantile Exchange

| | | |
|---|---|---|
| Feeder cattle | Deutsche mark | European currency |
| Live cattle | Canadian dollar | Treasury bill |
| Live hogs | French franc | Domestic CD |
| Pork bellies | Swiss franc | Eurodollar |
| Lumber | British pound | Gold |
| | Japanese yen | S&P 500 Stock Index |
| | Australian dollar | S&P 100 |
| | | S&P over the counter |

## Chicago Rice and Cotton Exchange

Rough rice

## Coffee, Sugar and Cocoa Exchange (New York)

| | | |
|---|---|---|
| Cocoa | World sugar | Inflation rate |
| Coffee | Sugar #14 | Consumer Price Index |
| | White sugar | |

## Commodity Exchange Inc. (New York)

| | |
|---|---|
| Aluminum | Silver |
| Copper | Gold |

## Kansas City Board of Trade

| | | |
|---|---|---|
| Wheat | Value Line Stock Index | Mini Value Line |

## Mid-America Commodity Exchange (Chicago)

| | | |
|---|---|---|
| Live cattle | New York gold | British pound |
| Live hogs | New York silver | Canadian dollar |
| Corn | Platinum | Deutsche mark |

TABLE 4-2.  U.S. FUTURES CONTRACTS *(continued)*.

| Oats | U.S. Treasury bond | Japanese yen |
|---|---|---|
| Soybeans | U.S. Treasury bill | Swiss franc |
| Soybean meal | | |
| Wheat | | |

### Minneapolis Grain Exchange

| Cotton No. 2 | U.S. Dollar Index | U.S. Treasury note |
|---|---|---|
| Orange juice | European Currency Unit | |

### New York Futures Exchange

| NYSE Composite Stock Index | Russell 2,000 Index |
|---|---|
| CRB Futures Price Index | Russell 3,000 Index |

### New York Mercantile Exchange

| Palladium | No. 2 heating oil | Crude oil |
|---|---|---|
| Platinum | Unleaded gasoline | Propane |

Source: *Futures Magazine.*

the world can communicate price quotes and other information almost instantaneously with any other part of the world.

This means that a hedger in Singapore can engage in a futures transaction in Chicago in real time. The only problem is the difference in time zones. To alleviate that problem, exchanges have begun to expand trading hours. In September 1987, the CBOT broke with tradition by adding evening trading hours—5:00 P.M. to 8:30 P.M. CST, Sunday through Thursday. Now, during business hours in the Far East, trading can be accomplished in U.S. Treasury bonds, U.S. Treasury notes, gold and silver through the Chicago pits.

Other exchanges are following suit. At the Philadelphia Board of Trade, several currencies can be traded during the hours of 7:00 P.M. to 11:00 P.M. EST, Sunday through Thursday. At this writing, the Philadelphia Board of Trade and its parent, the Philadelphia Stock Exchange, have been discussing expanding to a 20-hour trading format, from 7:00 P.M. to 3:00 P.M.

### Electronic Trading

A 20-hour schedule, of course, can exhaust the humans who must stand in the pits for long hours, noisily auctioning contracts. The futures industry, however, stands at the door of another era in its development. Computerized equipment now exists, which makes it possible to trade completely electronically, allowing traders to remain at their homes or offices, trading via computer screen and satellite linkage. Several contracts are now being traded in this manner, with more being developed. Not only that, but four exchanges are now completely mechanized, with no trading being done in the pits: the Stockholm Options Market, the Swiss Options and Financial Futures Exchange, the New Zealand Futures Exchange, and the International Futures Exchange in Bermuda.

I am convinced that such equipment will make the floor trader and the open outcry system obsolete within a few years. At that time, most financial futures will be traded 24 hours per day by electronic transmission in exchanges around the world.

### International Exchanges

Futures exchanges worldwide are currently being built or expanding services at an amazing rate. The trend is to link contracts with other exchanges for mutual offset—that is, a contract in one exchange can be offset by a position in another exchange. At this writing, U.S. Treasury bonds, Eurodollars, and Japanese bonds are all traded around the clock at various foreign and domestic exchanges. In 1986, the Japanese government bond futures on the Tokyo Stock Exchange surpassed the volume of the T-bond futures contract at the CBOT, making it the most actively traded futures contract in the world.

Table 4-3 lists all the foreign exchanges as well as the contracts traded on each. The newest is the computerized Swiss Options and Financial Futures Exchange (SOFFEX).

TABLE 4-3.  INTERNATIONAL FUTURES EXCHANGES.

### Toronto Futures Exchange (Canada)

| | |
|---|---|
| Canadian bond | TSE Oil and Gas Index |
| Canadian T-bill | U.S. dollar |
| Toronto Stock Exchange 300 Index | Toronto 35 Index |
| Toronto Stock Exchange 300 Spot Index | |

### Winnipeg Commodity Exchange (Canada)

| | |
|---|---|
| Domestic feed barley | Conola/rapeseed |
| Alberta domestic feed barley | Rye |
| Flaxseed | Domestic feed wheat |
| Domestic feed oats | Gold |

### Baltic Futures Exchange (London)

### Baltic International Freight Futures Exchange

### Baltic Freight Index

### London Grain Futures Market

| | |
|---|---|
| EEC wheat | EEC barley |

### London Meat Futures Exchange

| | |
|---|---|
| Live cattle | Pigs |

### London Potato Futures Market

Potatoes

### Soybean Meal Futures Association

Soybean meal

### International Petroleum Exchange of London Ltd.

| | |
|---|---|
| Gas oil (No. 2 heating oil) | Premium leaded gasoline |
| Heavy fuel oil | Crude oil |

*(continued)*

TABLE 4-3. INTERNATIONAL FUTURES EXCHANGES *(continued).*

| *London Futures and Options Exchange* | |
| --- | --- |
| Cocoa No. 6 | Sugar No. 6 (raw) |
| Coffee | Sugar No. 5 (white) |

| *London International Financial Futures Exchange* | |
| --- | --- |
| 20-year U.K. gilt interest Rate | Swiss franc |
| Short gilt | Japanese yen |
| 3-month Eurodollar interest rate | Dollar-mark currency |
| 3-month sterling interest rate | U.S. Treasury bond |
| British pound | Financial Times Stock Exchange 100 Index |
| Deutsche mark | Japanese government bond |

| *London Metal Exchange* | |
| --- | --- |
| Aluminum | Nickel |
| Copper (grade A) | Silver (10,000 troy oz.) |
| Copper (standard) | Silver (2,000 troy oz.) |
| Lead | Zinc |

| *Brazilian Futures Exchange* | |
| --- | --- |
| Gold | OTN–Nominal Treasury bond |
| Deutsche mark | CD |
| Japanese yen | IBV–blue chip (Rio de Janeiro Stock Exchange Index) |
| U.S. dollar | LBC (Central Bank bill) |

| *Sao Paulo Commodities Exchange* | | |
| --- | --- | --- |
| Cattle | Soybean bread | Japanese yen |
| Feeder cattle | Soybean oil | Brazilian CD |
| Cotton | Gold | |
| Coffee | U.S. dollar | |
| Soybeans | Deutsche mark | |

*(continued)*

### *Bolsa Mercantile & de Futures (Brazil)*

| | |
|---|---|
| Stock Index | U.S. dollar inflation |
| Gold | Deutsche mark |
| Coffee | Domestic CD |

### *Financiele Termijn Market Amsterdam (FTA)*

FTA Index

### *Hong Kong Futures Exchange*

| | |
|---|---|
| Sugar | Gold |
| Soybeans | Hong Seng Index |

### *International Futures Exchange (Bermuda)*
#### *(electronic trading system)*

| | |
|---|---|
| Baltic Freight Index | Financial News Composite Index |

### *Kuala Lumpur Commodity Exchange*

| | |
|---|---|
| Crude palm oil | Rubber |

### *Marche à Terme des Instruments Financiers de Paris*

| | |
|---|---|
| French government national bond | French Treasury 90-day bill |

### *New Zealand Futures Exchange*
#### *(electronic trading system)*

| | |
|---|---|
| U.S. dollar | Five-year government stock |
| New Zealand crossbred wool | 90-day back bills |
| | Barclays Share Price Index |

### *Osaka Securities Exchange*

Osaka Stock Futures 50

### *Paris Futures Exchange*

| | |
|---|---|
| White sugar | Coffee |
| Cocoa | Cocoa butter |

*(continued)*

TABLE 4-3. INTERNATIONAL FUTURES EXCHANGES *(continued)*.

---

### *Singapore International Monetary Exchange*

| | |
|---|---|
| Eurodollar (linked to CME) | British pound (linked to CME) |
| Japanese yen (linked to CME) | Nikkei Stock Average |
| Deutsche mark | U.S. Treasury bonds |
| Gold | |

### *Stockholm Options Market (electronic trading system)*

OMX Index

### *Swedish Options and Futures Exchange*

SX 16 Share Index

### *Swiss Options and Financial Futures Exchange (SOFFEX) (electronic trading system)*

| | |
|---|---|
| Options on Swiss stocks | Financial futures |
| Stock Index futures | |

### *Sydney Futures Exchange*

| | |
|---|---|
| Live cattle | Australian dollar |
| Wool | All Ordinaries Share Price Index |
| | Gold (linked to COMEX) |
| | 10-year Treasury bond |
| 90-day Bank bills of exchange | U.S. Treasury bonds (linked to LIFFE) |

### *Tokyo Stock Exchange*

Japanese yen bond

*Source: Futures Magazine.*

# CHAPTER 5

# Life on the Trading Floor

The business of the modern futures exchange is transacted on the trading floor, where hundreds of individuals gather each day for the purpose of exchanging futures contracts. Amid a steady din of voices crying out bids and offers, various clerks and runners scurry here and there with orders to be filled and orders to be reported. The scene is noisy, colorful, frenetic, and exciting—quite unlike anything that most people have experienced.

A friend of mine who worked for a while on the floor at both the Chicago Board of Trade (CBOT) and the Chicago Mercantile Exchange (CME) would often tell me

stories about his experiences there. I particularly remember the vivid description of his first day at the CME,
also known as the Merc:

> I waited by the reception desk while they paged my
> new floor supervisor. From the desk, I looked up at two
> long escalators carrying a steady stream of people up and
> down. There were people going up the escalator on the
> right wearing winter coats and jackets, with hats and
> gloves and purses and bags. They could have been at
> Sears or any other large downtown department store.
> Coming down the other escalator, everyone was wearing
> a bright-colored sportscoat. The predominant color was
> gold, although I saw light green, dark blue, and light blue
> interspersed among them.
>
> All the men wore ties, although very few were pulled
> up tightly around their necks. All of the jackets had
> picture ID cards clipped to the lapels, which they would
> unclip and run through a slot in the turnstyle to gain
> entrance to what I presumed to be the trading floor. It
> was as if all the people going up the escalator were being
> processed through a room where their normal street iden-
> tity was removed and they were issued uniform jackets
> that made them each a member of some kind of exclusive
> club.
>
> As I marveled at this transformation that was oc-
> curring to such a multitude of individuals, my new boss
> approached me. He came the opposite direction through
> one of those same turnstyles that were measuring with
> mechanical precision the flow of bright jackets from the
> escalator into the corridors leading to the trading floor.
> He was wearing a dark blue jacket.
>
> I figured dark blue must mean authority. There were
> very few of them around. And they came up from the
> floor below, rather than down with the horde. He had a
> larger badge, too, with three large letters on it. As I looked,
> I saw that it was a member's badge. I was impressed.
>
> My new boss sent me up the escalator with some
> papers, looking for the processing room. Soon, I was riding
> the escalator back down, with a picture ID clipped to the
> lapel of my fresh gold jacket. I was in the club.

When I zipped my ID badge through the slot in the turnstyle, a small light turned green, granting me entrance. A guard in a smart brown suit watched me push on the metal bar, which gave easily to my shove, clicking softly as it turned. I was inside, headed for the doors that marked the boundary of the trading floor.

As I pulled open the glass door, I was overwhelmed by the noise that suddenly confronted me. I immediately jumped to the conclusion that something quite significant must have happened, and a lot of people were mad about it, because here and there all over this huge room, groups of people were yelling at each other. With some hesitation, I walked in, only to find myself being pushed and jostled by various gold- and green-coated individuals who were hurrying around in what seemed to be a chaotic and disorganized confusion of aimless activity.

I fully expected a fight to break out at any moment.

To the uninitiated, it is totally incomprehensible that millions of dollars worth of business could be transacted everyday, in exchanges around the world, in such a primitive manner. In an era of computers, instant worldwide communication, mushrooming technological advancement, ultrasophisticated marketing techniques, international corporate conglomerates, arbitrageurs, and proliferating MBAs, the trading floor seems an anachronism—a throwback. And so it is.

The trading floor at the modern futures exchange is little removed from the open-air auctions and livestock sales of a century or more ago. Although monitored and reported by state-of-the-art electronics, the trading pit is nothing more than a process of offering a price for, or asking a price for, a specific commodity. The rules require it be done with open outcry.

Naturally, if business is to be transacted in a fair and consistent manner under such conditions, there must be other rules as well, and there are. The procedures are clearly spelled out; the limits are clearly established. The roles of the various characters in this intense daily drama of intrigue, excitement, subterfuge, and deal making are clearly written. And the system works remarkably well.

## THE PIT

At the heart of the open outcry market system is the *pit*, a circular construction forming just what the name implies: a hole in the trading floor. Concentric rings form steps, which flow from the outside of the pit toward the center, and upon which the floor traders stand, each a little higher than or lower than the trader in front or behind.

The highest step is above the floor level, so that one must first walk up two or three steps before walking down into the pit.On these outer steps, leading down from the top, stand clerks in gold jackets—assistants to the floor brokers. On the inside steps, leading down toward the sunken center of the pit, stand the floor brokers and the *locals*—traders who work for themselves—making trade after trade all day long, hoping to scalp a small profit from each trade.

Each pit is divided into pie-shaped wedges, with the nearby contract month always located in a particular area and the back months located in declining order around the pit. When a contract month expires, all the other contract months move up, so that, for example, the area that was formerly February pork bellies would become March bellies when the February contract expires, and so forth. Figure 5-1 is a diagram of the live cattle pit at the Chicago Mercantile Exchange, showing each of the areas of the pit. When the *front month* (or *spot month*) contract expires, each of the *back months* moves counterclockwise one spot, as shown.

### The Floor Broker

The floor broker, or pit broker, is a member of the exchange who has a business relationship with one or more brokerage firms. Most of the trading he or she does during trading hours is to fill orders that are brought into the pit by runners who work for the brokerage houses. At any one time, a pit broker will have a stack of orders in his or her hand, arranged in order of price and divided into buy orders and sell orders. Many brokers have so many orders that they employ clerks, or *deck holders,* to help hold the orders and keep them in order. These deck holders stand on the outside steps of the pit, with their backs to the inside of the pit. It is not uncommon for brokers who work the very busy contract months to have three or four clerks working for them.

Each of the pit brokers wears a distinctively colored jacket with his or her ID badge prominently displayed. On the badge are three to five large letters that identify the broker to other traders in the pit. When a trade is completed, these identifying letters appear on the order form as an endorsement, along with the letters identifying the trader who took the other side of the trade. Each set of letters is unique, so there is no chance to mistake who made the trade.

Most floor brokers handle orders for only one contract month, particularly if they work in one of the nearby contract months, where volume can be very high. In some of the very high-volume pits, a broker may handle only the buy orders for one contract month while another broker handles the sell orders. Other brokers handle only spread orders. By specializing in this manner, a broker ends up working in one particular spot in the pit day after day, making him or her easy to find when an order needs to be filled quickly.

### The Floor Trader

The locals are the traders who give liquidity to the market. Trading only for themselves, they make trade after trade, often taking the opposite side of a trade with one of the brokers, then exiting that trade in a few minutes when the price moves a few ticks. Often called *scalpers,* the locals rarely hold a position overnight, even

*Figure 5–1.  Diagram of the Live Cattle Pit, Chicago Mercantile Exchange.*

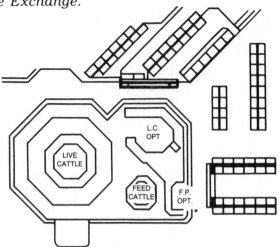

though they may have made dozens of trades during the day. In some of the high-volume pits, like the T-bonds at the CBOT or the S&P 500 at the CME, a local will stand in the same spot in the pit all day long, shoulder to shoulder with other traders, with still more traders in front and back, using his or her hands to signal a bid or an offer (a bid to buy is made with the palms turned in, toward the trader's own chest, while an offer to sell is made with the palms turned out, toward the other trader). Standing in the pit is not unlike being in the middle of a crowd leaving a football game or a rock concert, with people crowding against you, jostling you, pushing you, and breathing down your neck. It can be very warm and quite uncomfortable, as your feet grow tired and sore and your throat becomes dry and hoarse. Toward the end of a six- or seven-hour day, the job does not seem nearly as glamorous as most people assume it to be. In fact, working in a trading pit is a very basic, physically demanding, emotionally draining, competitive job.

A trader must keep his or her senses sharp even when six hours of tumult, noise, yelling, negotiating, and general confusion have dulled them to the point of being sluggish. Rushing adrenalin must certainly be a factor in maintaining a trader through a brutal trading day. The exchange keeps oxygen handy for the occasional trader who is physically overcome by the entire situation.

### Layout of the Trading Floor

Figure 5-2, a diagram of the trading floor at the CME, is typical of the layout of a large futures exchange. Notice that the meats are in one area, the currencies in another, the financials in a third. The space around the pits is often clogged with runners, clerks, and assorted other people moving at a feverish pace. Around the perimeter of the floor and in certain locations around the pits are rows of telephone desks, where phone clerks receive orders from their respective order rooms to be delivered to the pit brokers. At one corner of the floor are located the various news services, such as Reuters and Dow Jones, that are available for the trader's use.

High above the trading floor, on each wall of the trading room, are the *quote boards*, where the tick-by-tick price appears for each contract of each commodity. On the quote board, the most recent price appears at the bottom of a column of prices, with the next previous price above that and the five previous prices in order above that (see Figure 5-3). As a trade is made, the new price appears at the bottom, and the other prices move up, with the top price dropping off. The quote board also gives the previous day's settlement price and the high-low of the day's trading, along with the opening range, the year's high and low, and the net difference between the last price and the previous day's settlement price. Figure 5-3 is an example of how the quote board might appear in the trading room.

### How An Order Is Filled

To the uninitiated, it seems almost miraculous that one small order for one futures contract from a trader somewhere in Idaho could actually be filled at a good

*Figure 5–2.* Diagram of the Trading Floor, Chicago
Mercantile Exchange.

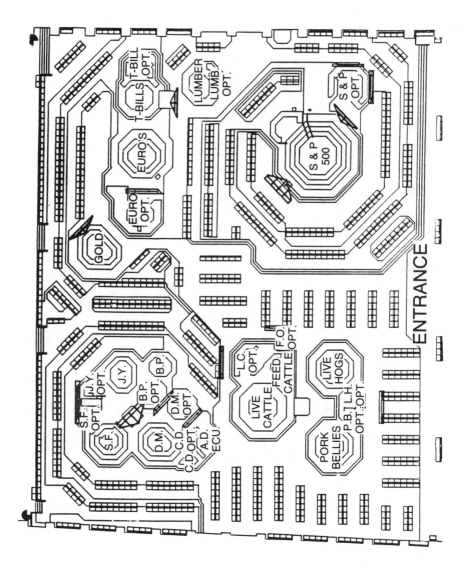

TABLE 5.3. QUOTE BOARD.

| Market and month symbol | SN | SQ | SU | SX | SF |
|---|---|---|---|---|---|
| Open | 7030 | 6830 | 6500 | 6340 | 6380 |
| High | 7140 | 6870 | 6540 | 6370 | 6430 |
| Low | 6984 | 6790 | 6464 | 6280 | 6360 |
| Last | 7100 | 6844 | 6504 | 6320 | 6394 |
| Net change for day | −10 | −70 | −120 | −142 | −146 |

price and in a reasonable time in the midst of all the chaos on the trading floor. And yet, that's exactly what happens day in and day out. The trader in Idaho may call his or her broker with an order to buy one contract of live hogs at the market. The broker may be a discount broker in Chicago or a local broker in his or her hometown. That broker then relays the order to a phone clerk on the trading floor. The process for relaying the order will vary from broker to broker. Some have central order rooms to whom the broker gives the order. Others have a hotline direct to the floor. At each stage, the order is taken on a recorded phone and time stamped. When it arrives at the trading floor, the phone clerk there writes the order and hands it to a runner, who quickly carries the order to the appropriate pit broker. The order is either given directly to the broker or to the broker's clerk (the deckholder).

Because the order is a market order, the broker will bid the appropriate price, depending on the price at which live hogs have been trading. If he or she does not get a response at that price, the bid is made at a higher price, until the order is filled.

The runner, knowing the order is a market order, has waited for the fill, so as soon as the pit broker endorses the order, he or she returns it to the runner, who carries the filled order immediately to the phone clerk, who calls the broker who phoned in the order to give him or her the price fill. At each step of the fill confirmation, the order is again time stamped.

If the order is a price order, it is simply delivered to the broker or the clerk, who then places it in the appropriate spot in the deck. Later, if the order is filled, it is returned to a runner, who carries the order back to a phone clerk, who then confirms the fill with the broker. At the end of the day, all unfilled orders that have not been designated good till canceled are voided.

In many of the currency and financial pits, orders are filled in a somewhat different manner. When the order is phoned in, the phone clerk, through a set of hand signals called *arbing,* or *arbitraging,* flashes the order to an arb clerk, who then conveys the order orally to the broker in the pit. As soon as the order is filled, the arb clerk flashes the signal back to the phone clerk who often has the retail broker still on the line and confirms the fill immediately. The written order is then carried into the pit by a runner so that the broker can endorse it later.

## THE BID AND THE OFFER

The first question asked by most people when encountering the trading floor for the first time is, "How does anybody know what's going on in all that confusion?" Fortunately, a set of rules and procedures—some formal, some informal—govern the activity so that business can be transacted efficiently.

In the open outcry system, a trader in the pit must communicate his or her intentions as prices move very fast and trades occur very rapidly. To accomplish that, a code has been developed that is easily understood and communicated. As we have already learned, the only part of a contract that is negotiated in the pit is price. Everything else is standardized. Therefore, the trader in the pit need communicate only three things: (1) whether he or she wishes to buy or sell; (2) the number of contracts he or she wishes to trade; and (3) the price. The contract month is known because of the location in the pit where the trader is standing.

Let's say a trader is willing to pay $8.30¼ for two contracts of November soybeans. All the other traders in the pit know that soybeans are trading at $8.30, so the trader only needs to mention the one-quarter cent. If the trader means to say, "I'll pay $8.30¼ for two November soybeans," then all he or she needs to yell is "quarter for 10" (there are 5,000 bushels of soybeans in a contract, commonly shortened to 5; two contracts would be 10). If, on the other hand, the trader wishes to sell three contracts of soybeans at $8.30½, rather than yell, "I'll sell 15,000 bushels of November soybeans at $8.30½," he or she simply yells "15 at a half."

Along with yelling the bid or offer, the trader also uses hand signals at the same time. With arms outstretched to get attention, the palms face in if the trader wishes to buy and out if the trader wishes to sell.

## HOW PRICES REACH THE QUOTE BOARD

At the CME, a pit observer, who is an employee of the exchange, stands in the pit with a walkie-talkie. Each time the price changes, the observer radios the information into the CME operator, who enters the information into the CME Quote Entry System. The price immediately appears on the quote board and is simultaneously broadcast on the CME ticker to the public. Thus, traders who have the equipment to receive ticker information and who have paid the necessary subscription fees receive price quotes at the same time they appear on the quote board.

There are times, however, when trading volume is so high that the quote entry system cannot keep up. At those times, the board will note that it is a fast market and will only display four prices rather than the usual seven.

At each of the individual brokerage-house desks around the floor of the exchange is a *floor manager,* or *floor supervisor.* As the name implies, the floor manager is in charge of the operations at the desk, seeing that orders are handled with dispatch and with care. If disputes arise over price fees, the floor manager is the first line person to try to resolve the difference. Basically, it is the job of the floor manager to see that everything runs smoothly around the desk.

Many of the larger brokerage houses will have *market analysts* on the floor at all times. These are market veterans who watch closely what is happening in the pit, reporting on who's buying and who's selling and why. Often, their reports will go out periodically to the retail brokerage offices around the country so that brokers can report up-to-the-minute developments to their clients.

Each of the brokerage houses also employ *out-trade clerks.* At the close of trading each day, it is the job of each trader to match all the trades from the day's activity and to clear them through the clearinghouse. With all the activity that goes on in the pit during trading hours, however, it is not uncommon for errors to be made. One floor broker may have registered a trade with another floor broker, only to find that the second broker has no record of the trade. This is called an *out trade.* Naturally, the customer has already been given a fill, so a match must be found somewhere so that the trade can be cleared.

It is the job of the out-trade clerk to find that match. Often, the problem is simply that the wrong ID was written on the order form when the broker endorsed it or that the wrong price was noted on a local's trading card. At other times, there is another out trade on the opposite side that can be matched with the first one. Whatever the solution, it is the out-trade clerk's job to find it because no outstanding trade can be allowed to remain uncleared until the next day's trading.

Consequently, each day before the markets open, the out-trade clerks from the various brokerage houses meet in one of the pits, computer printouts in hand, taking care of all the trades that the computer has been unable to match. After particularly high-volume days, it is not uncommon for the out-trade clerks to arrive at 3:00 or 4:00 A.M. to take care of all the out trades before the start of trading.

# CHAPTER 6

# The Basics of Trading Futures

An individual who wishes to trade commodity futures must make several crucial decisions before he or she begins. One of the most critical of these decisions is the choice of a broker.

## CHOOSING A BROKER

Only a few years ago, the choice was less difficult than at present. Prior to the 1960s, there were not many firms to choose from, and all seemed to offer about the same service. But then, during the 1960s, brokerage firms tended to develop a specialty; some were thought to be particularly adept at metals, for example, while others were especially good at tropicals. Customers expected their broker to have an inside line on the commodity and therefore gave great credence to the broker's advice. In fact, most people who speculated in commodities during that era did so on the basis of their broker's recommendations, believing that a good broker was the key to making profits in commodities.

During the 1970s, however, two developments occurred that significantly altered the broker-client relationship. The first was the de facto deregulation of brokerage commissions, which led to a brutal commission war and the proliferation of discount brokerage firms. The second was the decrease in futures trading volume in the traditional markets and the corresponding surge of volume in the financial and currencies markets. No longer did firms have a specialty and thereby attract and retain a certain loyal clientele. Not only that, but an ever-growing number of speculators were relying on their own technical analysis of the markets rather than their brokers' advice. To these individuals, a commission rate that was one-half or one-third that of the full-service broker was very attractive.

As a consequence of these developments in the futures industry, however, the process of choosing a commodities broker has become both complex and confusing. Far too often, the method seems to follow the pattern as shown in the following paragraphs.

Alice, an attorney, has lunch with a colleague who spins a gripping tale told her by a friend she spoke with over cocktails at a party the previous Friday night. The colleague's friend, it seems, had been watching interest rates and the T-bond market quite closely, and he knew the bonds were ready to make a big move. He opened a small account with a broker, bought a contract of bonds, and five days later had doubled his money.

A week later, Alice is at a cocktail party and strikes up a conversation with a stranger who talks at length about the declining value of the dollar. After a stunning display of financial expertise, he concludes the discourse by saying, "I'm fully invested right now, unfortunately, but if I had some extra cash I'd open an account with a discount firm and buy some Swiss francs."

By now, it has become obvious to Alice that there are people who have an insight into the various markets and that if she can tap into that she might make a lot of money. On her way to the office one morning shortly thereafter, she relieves the boredom of the train ride by glancing through the business section of the newspaper. Sure enough, there are columnists writing with glib confidence about the balance of trade, the deficit, the direction of interest rates, and the value of the dollar on international markets. Just before the train arrives downtown, Alice tears out a coupon from a brokerage firm ad and stuffs it into her purse. Later, at the office, she fills out the ad and mails it.

Less than a week later, Alice receives a phone call from the broker in the ad. He determines that Alice is a novice, with approximately $5,000 to risk, who is interested in speculating in bonds or Swiss francs, depending on how they are doing right now. "Well, Alice," the broker responds, "I'm particularly bullish on soybeans right now. We've been having a dry spring, and I think they could go to $9.00 in the next week or two. The bonds and francs have been too choppy lately, so I don't see a good trade there."

After covering two more good reasons to buy soybeans, the broker agrees to send Alice some account forms, which she receives two days later. Glancing quickly through the disclaimers that caution her about the risk of significant losses, she fills out the forms, makes out a check, and mails the package back to the broker. Two days later, she receives a call from the broker to verify the information on the account forms and to let her know that he will call as soon as the right trade presents itself. Alice, of course, has been watching the price of beans on her train ride to work every morning and knows they have indeed been going up.

One day later, the broker calls with a recommendation to buy November beans at a price of $7.60 a bushel. Alice quickly agrees, and the broker places the order. Five minutes later, the phone rings, and the broker informs her, "You bought 5,000 bushels of November soybeans at $7.65 a bushel." Alice is ecstatic.

Unfortunately, Alice is very likely to have a bad experience in the commodities market because of the haphazard manner in which she selected her broker. It is highly unlikely that she would plunk down $5,000 so easily for any other reason. The successful attorney that she is, she would be very careful about buying a used $5,000 automobile, carefully selecting the dealer to buy from, having the car inspected by a mechanic friend, checking the blue book of car prices, reading through the annual used car issue of *Consumer Reports* magazine. Yet, without hesitation, she just sent $5,000 to a voice on the phone. If Alice wanted to be as careful about selecting a broker as she would be about buying a car, what should she do?

*Rules for Selecting a Broker*

*Rule #1:* A would-be speculator in commodity futures must first decide what kind of trader he or she is or would like to be. In today's market, there are four general categories of traders:

1. The novice. This trader has little or no experience or knowledge of futures trading, is probably nervous, uncertain and insecure, and requires a broker who is patient, not too busy, and familiar with the details that concern the novice trader, such as appropriate placement of orders, margin requirements, understanding purchase and sale statements, contract specifications, reports, and an elementary knowledge of various trading systems.

2. The experienced short-term trader. This is usually an individual with considerable experience and mar-

ket knowledge who is interested in making intra-day trades or trades that will last only a few days. Such a person may want price quotes and other information from the broker, but basically he or she requires a broker who can execute orders promptly, efficiently, and at reasonably good prices.

3. The long-term trader. Generally, a long-term position trader uses fundamental knowledge of the commodities he or she trades in to take a position and hold it for a relatively long time. This trader would do well to use a brokerage firm that can provide correct statistical and fundamental data.

4. The independent trader. This trader desires absolutely no input from the broker and works best with a broker who is primarily an order taker.

*Rule #2:* The would-be trader must survey the available brokerage firms and determine what services each provides. There are two broad categories of brokers: the full-service broker and the discount broker, although the difference is growing less distinct as time passes.

1. The full-service broker. This is the traditional type of brokerage firm that provides virtually any financial service including stocks, bonds, futures, money market funds, tax shelters, options, research publications, and so forth. Some full-service brokers handle both stocks and commodities, while others provide such services in the area of futures trading only. A full-service futures broker will provide considerable research, will offer price quotes, will give trading advice and assist the customer in making trading decisions, and may offer discretionary and managed account programs.

2. The discount broker. These brokers do not provide costly research and research publications, nor do they help the client develop a strategy or provide trading advice beyond the most basic. They simply fill the orders

and meet the reporting and financial obligations of a broker, such as trade confirmations and purchase and sale statements. In recent years, however, some discount brokers have begun offering a sliding scale of commissions, based on a selection of optional services such as research and broker assistance, usually at a rate less than the full-service houses charge. Likewise, many full-service firms are offering discounted services to clients who do not require broker assistance, price quotations, and market research.

*Rule #3:* When selecting a brokerage firm, the speculator must be certain that his or her capital will be safe. The best way to do this is to obtain references and be certain that the firm has backing.

*Rule #4:* The trader should compare commission rates. It is important, however, not to make a decision based solely on the price of commissions. After deciding on the services required (Rule #1), the trader must be prepared to pay a reasonable fee for those services.

*Rule #5:* If possible, the trader should visit the brokers' offices before making a final decision. A great deal can be learned from such a visit.

*Rule #6:* A trader who will rely on recommendations from the broker should check the broker's track record. How good is this broker at calling winning trades? How many clients have ended up losing all or most of their money from following this broker's advice? A track record may be difficult to pin down, but asking the right questions can provide useful information. It must be remembered that the vast majority of traders who trade small accounts on their broker's advice lose money.

*Rule #7:* The prospective trader must not have unrealistic expectations about a broker. My book *The Investor's Quotient* makes the assertion that every broker should be expected to carry out the following functions:

*1.* Take and execute all orders promptly and accurately.

*2.* Report back promptly and accurately on all order fills.

*3.* Keep the client informed of news if he or she so desires.

*4.* Maintain and report account balances, margins, and other financial details.

*5.* Be available and on call each and every time the client wishes to place an order.

*6.* Keep abreast of important changes in costs, commissions, margins, legal details, and the like, and inform the client as necessary.

*7.* Obtain market information (the bid-and-ask price, the early price call, the volume of contracts being traded, etc.) upon request.

*Rule #8:* It must be remembered that a broker makes his or her money by commission. Therefore, the more trades that are made, the more money the broker makes. On the other hand, if he or she recommends too many trades, they may burn the account out too quickly, thus losing the account. The important thing to remember is that the client's interests are often secondary to the broker's interests. In conversation with a prospective broker and through recommendations, the aspiring trader must attempt to ascertain the broker's performance in light of this consideration.

So now that we know the procedure Alice should have followed in selecting her broker, let's take a look at what happened to her after she followed none of the eight rules but instead rather impulsively sent $5,000 to a firm she knew nothing about. First, the broker she selected was correct in his assertion that soybeans would go up. In fact, less than two weeks after Alice bought her beans at $7.65, the price of soybeans was trading as high as $8.65. Since each one cent change in soybeans is worth $50, Alice should have made $5,000 on her trade.

Unfortunately for Alice, however, the day after she bought her soybeans, the price dropped 30 cents, which is the limit that the soybean market can move in one trading day. (This is called a limit move.) The next day, prices stabilized but did not bounce back. Alice's account was now worth only $3,500. In a panic, she called her broker, who assured her that such short-term moves are not uncommon, that this one occurred because a local weather forecaster predicted rain—a prediction that did not materialize.

The third day of Alice's trading career, a rumor of rain again swept the market and the price once more dropped 30 cents. Alice now had only $2,000 left. Again she called her broker. "What's going on?" she demanded. "You said this was a sure thing, and here I am losing all my money. I was counting on that money for a vacation I'm planning, and now it's almost gone!"

In a calm, reassuring voice the broker told Alice that things should turn around soon, but just in case they didn't perhaps she should put a stop-loss order in. In effect, this stop-loss order instructed the floor broker to liquidate Alice's position if the price of soybeans dropped to $7. Having no one to rely on but the broker, Alice agreed and then waited.

The next day, the price of beans opened unchanged—a good sign. In the next half hour, the price crept up slowly. When Alice called her broker at 10:00 A.M., the price stood at $7.10. The broker was certain that prices would continue to go up, based on a long-term weather forecast of continued drought. But then, something strange happened. Prices began to fall again. An order to sell a large quantity of soybeans had come into the pit, driving prices down. From $7.10, they went to $7.08, then $7.05, then $7.03. At $6.98, the slide ended, and prices began to rise again. By the end of the day, prices stood at $7.35, a limit up move. The broker was right! They did recover!

But Alice did not profit from the rise. When prices dropped to $7, the floor broker had dutifully filled her order to sell, thus taking Alice out of the market. Her net loss was $3,250.

The next morning, in shock and depressed, Alice did two things. First, she called the broker and asked him to send her the remaining $1,750, which he did, minus the $125 commission charge. Finally, Alice called her travel agent and canceled her travel plans.

Would things have turned out differently for Alice if she had been more careful in selecting a broker? That is difficult to say. Certainly, there are brokers who would have asked more questions about her investment goals as well as the source of her money, and most brokers would have cautioned Alice not to use vacation money to speculate with.

If Alice had shopped around for a broker, she might have had a better experience in commodities trading, or she might have decided not to trade at all, after she had learned the true risks involved. Then again, she might have continued to insist on plunking down her $5,000 and taking her chances. We will never know. The point to be made is that the broker-client relationship is critical to successful commodity trading, and it is essential that every active or would-be commodity trader carefully follow the rules I have presented for choosing a broker.

### Opening an Account

Once an aspiring commodities trader has decided on a suitable broker, the next step is to open an account. The paperwork is fairly simple and straightforward, and the broker will be more than happy to help with it. The forms to be filled out serve two essential purposes: to ascertain whether the individual is financially qualified to trade commodities and to obtain the individual's signature acknowledging the various risks involved in trading commodities.

In recent years, legislation that established the Commodity Futures Trading Commission (CFTC) and self-regulation by the National Futures Association (NFA) has led to a situation where every broker must be very concerned about the interests of the potential client. Thus, the process of establishing an account will likely include carefully worded disclaimers, which the client must sign, and a tape-recorded conversation, usually by phone, in which the broker qualifies the client by verifying the information included in the application form and determining that the client understands and acknowledges all the risks involved in futures trading.

When opening an account, the would-be futures trader faces another important decision: What size account should I establish? Is $1,000 enough? $5,000? Though seemingly a simple decision, research has shown that the size of a trading account has a direct relationship to success in futures trading. The fact is that most accounts of $5,000 or less lose money, just as Alice did in her brief foray into futures trading. In fact, it is not until account size reaches $15,000 that the odds of success become more realistic.

The reasons for this are inherent within the nature of futures trading. Consider that the best professional futures traders rarely achieve more than 50% accuracy in their trading. In other words, most successful traders lose money on more than half of their trades. Their success lies in being able to cut their losses short on each losing trade and to stay with the profitable trades long enough to offset all the small losses and thus show a net profit in the account. Once this is understood, it becomes apparent why an account of less than $15,000 is very risky. There is little room in such an account to withstand a series of small losses. Often, the account will be depleted before a profitable trade occurs. Similarly, as with Alice in our illustrative example, $5,000 does not allow a trader to stay with a high-conviction trade through a series of short-term opposing moves. If Alice had begun with $15,000, she might have been able to place her stop-loss at a point further away from the trading price, thus avoiding being stopped out of the market. If so, a losing trade would have turned into a very profitable trade.

## Contract Specifications

In an earlier chapter, the point was made that futures contracts are standardized by quantity, quality, and point of delivery. Because most futures traders never take delivery of the commodity, they do not need to be concerned with the quality and delivery point, except for understanding that it is standardized. The unit size of a contract is of concern, however, if only to avoid confusion when placing orders.

In this chapter, I will not attempt to cover every contract as to size and specifications. Rather, I have included in the Appendix a complete list of futures contracts, as of this printing, which provides all the information needed by a futures trader regarding a contract to be traded. For now, there are only two specific aspects of the standardized contract that I wish to focus on: the contract size designation and the *tick value* of the contract.

For hedgers, the size of a contract is of particular interest, since they must trade in sufficient quantities to cover their holdings of the commodity itself. For a speculator, the size of a contract is of little interest, except to note the difference between grain contracts and all other contracts. In the grains, which include oats, corn, wheat, and soybeans, a contract is for 5,000 bushels.

When placing an order in the grains, the trader will specify "buy (or sell) 5,000 bushels" of whatever grain is being traded. In shorthand, this becomes "buy five corn" (or wheat or oats or beans). It is important to remember that the number five here refers to one contract of 5,000 bushels. In every other contract, the number in the order refers to the quantity of contracts being traded—for example, "buy one Japanese yen."

The second aspect of the futures contract—the so-called tick value—is the most critical for the futures trader. In the chart in the Appendix, the tick value is called the *dollar value* of the *minimum fluctuation*. For the trader, this simply means how much one tick on the chart is worth.

Thus, if I am trading in cattle and I have a long position (I am a buyer) at $6.75, this means that I have a contract to buy 40,000 pounds of cattle at $6.75 per hundred weight, or 67.5 cents per pound. In cattle, the minimum fluctuation (one tick) is worth $10. This simply means that every time the price goes up one tick I make $10 (because I can then sell for $10 more than I paid). Likewise, every time the price goes down one tick, I lose $10. For each commodity, the tick value varies, so it is important for the trader to check before attempting a trade.

### Contract Months

One of the first things a new speculator will notice when attempting to trade commodity futures is that there are several different contracts available for each commodity, each designated by a certain month. The closest month is called the front, or the spot, month, whereas the further months are called the back months. Some contracts may be for as far away as 18 months while others may be due for delivery in the very next month from the one in which the trade is made.

In a normal market, the further a contract is from the spot month, the higher the price. This higher price represents the *carrying charge,* or the cost of holding a commodity in storage. Sometimes, however, the back month prices will be lower, creating an inverted market.

The highest volume of trading occurs in the front months, creating the most liquid market. Generally, the further a contract delivery is from the spot month, the less volume there is. For short-term or intra-day traders, then, the best month to trade in is the front month because of the liquidity of the market in this month. When a market lacks volume, or liquidity, it becomes more difficult to get in and out of the market at a desirable price. For longer-term position traders, the back months provide appropriate trading opportunities.

## PLACING AN ORDER

In futures trading the timing of a trade is a critical factor in determining the success or failure of the trade. In many of the futures markets, there is a great deal of volatility in price movement throughout the day. Thus, a trader who wishes to place an order might need to do so at a certain price in order to make a successful trade. Knowing how to get an order filled at a reasonably advantageous price is a critical factor in successful futures trading. Thus, knowing how to place an order with a broker is an essential skill for the would-be futures trader. Additionally, because the chance for error is so great in a fast-paced business like commodity trading, following the correct procedure for order placement is one way to avoid costly mistakes.

All order conversations are recorded, so that in the event of an error or a disputed order the tape can be played back to determine exactly what was said. If the trader made a mistake, then he or she is liable for the resulting expenses, whatever they may be. If the broker or order clerk makes the mistake, an adjustment will be made. Nobody can make up for missed opportunities or disadvantageous fills that occur because of trader ignorance or negligence, however. In every situation, the trader must insist that the person who takes the order repeats the order back before ending the phone call. Placing the order, then, is simply a matter of calling the broker and giving him or her the instructions. Giving the proper instructions, though, is crucial.

## TYPES OF ORDERS

*Market order.* The easiest order to place is the market order. It is simply an instruction to buy or sell at whatever price is being asked or bid in the pit when the order arrives there. The floor broker will execute such an order at the best possible price immediately upon

receiving it. In an active market, a market order is relatively safe and is quite commonly used. In a less active
market, however, this order should be used only when
it is vital to have the trade filled immediately because
the price at which the trade is completed can end up
being much higher or lower than the trader originally
intended.

If, for example, the order is to buy at the market,
but there are no price offers in the pit that are close to
the last trade, the floor broker will bid higher and higher
until the order is filled. The price fill received by the
trader may then be quite different from the expected
price.

*Market-not-held order.* This order can also be called
DRT (disregard tape). It is an instruction to the floor
broker to use his or her own discretion in filling the
order, so as to obtain the best price. Generally used with
large orders in a thin market, the DRT or not-held stipulation allows the broker to work the order rather than
simply dumping it into the pit and causing a large price
movement.

*Market-on-close (MOC) order.* A market-on-close order is an instruction to the floor broker to execute the
order during the last minute of trading at the end of the
trading day. In an active market, such an order can
result in a good fill, but it is not uncommon for a MOC
order to be filled several ticks away from the posted
closing price.

*Market-on-the-open order.* This is an instruction to
fill the order at the market price immediately on the
opening. The order, of course, goes into the floor broker
before the opening bell. Many traders feel that the opening is not a good reflection of market activity and so tend
to avoid such orders.

*Market-if-touched (MIT) order.* A market-if-touched
order is an instruction to execute the order at the market,
but only if a particular price is hit. For example, if the
order is to buy soybeans at $6.25 MIT, the order will be
activated only after $6.25 is actually asked. Then, the

broker will attempt to get the best price but at the market, which means the actual fill could be at a price quite higher than $6.25, depending on the market.

The MIT order is always placed above the market if it is a sell order and below the market if it is a buy order. This is only reasonable. A trader wants to sell for a higher price than is being bid or buy at a lower price than is being asked. That is the purpose of the MIT order. Remember, though, that the MIT order does not guarantee that the trade will be filled at the designated price. Once the price is hit, an MIT becomes a market order, and therefore it might be filled at a price worse than the specified price, particularly in a thin market.

*Limit order, or price order.* If a trader wishes to enter the market at a particular price, as with the MIT order, but will not accept a price that is worse than the designated price, then he or she must use a limit order. This tells the broker to fill the order at that price or better. If the order is to buy soybeans at $6.25, the broker must fill the order at $6.25 or lower. Conversely, if the order is to sell soybeans at $6.25, the broker must sell at $6.25 or higher.

When placing a limit order, the trader does not need to use the word "limit." It is sufficient to specify the price. The broker understands that it is a limit order and that the price given is the limit the trader is willing to bid or offer.

*Stop order.* A stop order is an order to buy if the price hits a specified level above the market or an order to sell if the price hits a specified level below the market. Stop orders are used for two purposes. One is to limit the risk of a particular trade by designating a price at which the position will be liquidated if the market moves the wrong way (stop-loss). The other is to enter the market after prices have gone beyond an identified price level.

*Buy-stop order.* This is an order to buy at a given price above the market. When the indicated price is hit, the order becomes a market order. That is, a buy-stop becomes an order to buy at the market if the price trades at or through the stop price or if the price is bid at or through the stop price. An actual trade need not occur to elect the stop. A bid at or through the stop price will elect the stop and make it a market order.

A buy-stop order can be used to enter a long position on market strength. As an example, if gold has been trading between $520 and $525 per ounce and a trader feels that once it goes beyond $525—a resistance point— the price will likely go much higher, a buy-stop would be placed just past $525, perhaps at $525.50. Thus, the trader would be in a position to catch the move if it occurs.

*Sell-stop order.* A sell-stop is an order to sell at a price below the market. As with the buy-stop order, the sell-stop becomes a market order if the price trades at or below the stop price or if the market is offered at or below the stop price. Once the stop is hit, the order is filled at the best possible price. As with the buy-stop, the price need not be traded, only offered, for the sell-stop to be elected. Such an order is used to enter a short position on market weakness.

*Stop-loss order.* The term "stop-loss" is a generic term applied to stop orders that are intended to limit loss. Such an order can be either buy-stop or sell-stop. A stop-loss order is entered concurrently to offset an existing position or another order. If a trader is long five contracts of soybeans at $7.83, let's say, but wants to limit his or her loss to $100 per contract, a sell-stop order would be entered at $7.81 (a one-cent move in soybeans is worth $50). If the market moves up, the stop-loss order will not be filled. If the market moves down, however, the order will be filled and the trader will be out of the market with a $500 loss ($100 × five contracts). The term "stop-loss" does not appear on the order, only the word "stop."

*Stop-limit order.* A stop-limit order is a combination of a stop order and a limit order. Whereas the normal stop order converts to a market order when the specified price is hit, a stop-limit order converts to a limit order.

With a stop-limit order, two prices are given: the stop price, which activates the order, and the limit price, which is the limit the trader is willing to accept. The order would look like this: "Buy five soybeans at $6.75 stop $6.74 limit."

A stop-limit order should not be used as a stop-loss, since the order has a chance of not being filled. The advantage of this kind of order is that the order will not be filled at any worse than the limit price; the disadvantage is that the order might not be filled at all if the market moves beyond the limit price before the floor broker can get the order filled.

*Stop-close-only order.* This is an instruction to sell or buy within the closing minute of trading. A sell-stop-close-only order will be executed at or below the given price during the closing minute, whereas a buy-stop-close-only will be executed at or above the given price. Often the fill price will not agree with the settlement price because of the time span during which the stop-close-only order can be filled.

*Or-better order.* There are times when a trader wants to enter a buy-limit order above the market or a sell-limit order below the market. Usually, such an order is placed only a few ticks away from the market and is entered for the purpose of catching a strong breakout. If, for example, silver is trading around $6.79 and the trader wants to catch what appears to be a strong rally, he or she does not want to risk placing a market order or a stop order (which becomes a market order when hit) because of the risk of being filled at too high a price. The most this trader is willing to pay is $6.81. The order would be placed "buy one silver at $6.81 or better (OB)." Without the specification OB, the broker or the broker's clerk would likely send the order back as a bad order (buy-limit orders are always placed below the market). With the specification OB, the clerk and the broker know what the trader intends.

Often, however, traders will mistakenly add the designation OB to a regular limit order. This is a tip-off to the broker that the trader is a novice and often will only antagonize the floor broker, who feels that he or she always tries to get the best possible price for the client without being told "or better."

*Fill-or-kill (FOK) order.* This order is not used very frequently. It is an instruction to the pit broker to fill the order immediately or to cancel the order. If the broker is unable to fill the order, he or she reports back "unable" and the order is cancelled (killed).

Such an order is used when a trader wishes to enter or exit a position quickly without the risk associated with a market order. FOK orders can be used in thin markets or in markets that have been hovering around a certain price level but for some reason will not come to the price level desired by the trader.

*Good-till-canceled (GTC) order.* This order, also known as an open order, remains in the pit until it is filled or until the trader cancels it. Most brokerage firms clear the books of all unfilled orders at the end of each trading day, except for those designated as open orders, or good till canceled. It is not uncommon for an open order to remain in the pit for several days, even weeks, although it is important for the trader to remember that an open order has been placed; otherwise he or she may receive a surprise some day of a fill they were not expecting.

*One-cancels-the-other (OCO) order.* At times, a trader wants to position himself or herself to catch a break regardless of the direction the market moves. For this purpose, two orders can be placed, one above the market, one below, with the stipulation that if one is filled, the other is canceled.

*Margin and margin call.* The term "margin," as it is used in commodity trading, is really a misnomer that has been carried over from stock trading. When a trader buys stock, he or she can borrow half the amount from the broker and put up the other half in cash. This is called a 50% margin, which is the limit brokers are allowed to offer. (In the 1920s, brokers were selling stock on 10% margin, which many believe contributed to the

1929 market crash.) In the futures market, a specified amount, also called margin, is deposited with the broker when a trade is made. This margin money, however, does not purchase anything. It simply serves as earnest money.

The trader has entered into a contract either to buy or sell a commodity at a future date. No sale has actually occurred, hence no money has been spent. If the market moves against the trader, the margin will be used to pay for the loss as the position declines in value. At a certain point, however, the margin money on deposit will be insufficient to cover additional losses, and the trader will be asked to deposit additional margin money or to liquidate the position and take the present loss.

Thus, for each commodity, there are two margin values established: initial margin and maintenance margin. Initial margin is the amount that must be on deposit in the account when a trade is initiated. Initial margin requirements vary substantially from commodity to commodity and are subject to change by the exchange depending on the volatility of the market. For example, in October 1987, immediately following the stock market crash, the margin for the S&P 500 contract was raised from $6,000 to $50,000 nearly overnight. The reason was the unprecedented price swings that were occurring, which often quickly exceeded the margin money many traders had on deposit.

Maintenance margin is the minimum amount that must be maintained in the account to hold a position. As a trade loses value, it erodes the amount of margin in the account. Once the account balance is below the established maintenance margin, the broker issues a margin call. The trader is obligated to deposit enough money in the account immediately to return the account to initial margin. Otherwise, the broker will liquidate the position.

Minimum margin requirements are established by the exchange. Individual brokers may, and often do, establish higher margins than the minimums, but they may not establish margins that are lower than the exchange minimums. Day trades—trades that will be exited by the end of the day—are not subject to margin requirements. Any position held past the end of the trading session, however, must be covered by the necessary margin amount.

*Short selling.* One of the most difficult concepts for the novice commodities trader to master is the idea of selling a commodity first, then buying it back later. "How can I sell something I don't own?" is the common complaint. Actually, the practice is not unique to futures trading.

To cite a very familiar example, consider what happens when a Girl Scout solicits orders for Girl Scout cookies during their annual fund drive. Essentially, when the Girl Scout takes an order for cookies, she has become a short seller. She has sold cookies she doesn't have, with the agreement that she will deliver the cookies at a later date. The same thing occurs at an automobile dealership when a customer orders a new car for later delivery. This time, however, the salesperson will likely demand a deposit—earnest money—before accepting the order. The salesperson has, however, sold a car he or she does not own, and which has not yet been built. The salesperson is "short" the car (in the same way a person might be "short" of cash). That salesperson, then, has become a short seller in a futures contract.

The difference between these two examples—the Girl Scout and the car salesperson—and futures trading is that delivery of the cookies and the car will likely occur, whereas delivery of a commodity futures contract rarely occurs. To avoid having to make delivery, the short seller can simply become a buyer of the same commodity in the same delivery month and offset the previous short position.

The same thing can happen in our example of the Girl Scout cookies. Perhaps, after the Girl Scout takes our order (she sells short), she turns the order over to the Girl Scout leader, who then arranges for delivery of the cookies and collection of money. By turning in the order (the contract), the Girl Scout has liquidated her position by transferring it to the leader, who is now the short seller. In the futures market, the trader who originally took a short position liquidates that position by taking an offsetting long position. The exchange functions exactly like the Girl Scout leader, in this case, by assuming delivery responsibility from the trader. The trader's profit or loss is the difference between the selling price and the buying price, minus commissions. The important point to remember, though, is that short selling, or taking a short position, can occur either to liquidate a previous long position or to take a new short position. The procedure is the same.

## COMMISSIONS

In the world of selling, sales commissions are a ubiquitous and easily understood practice. When a person sells an item or a service, he or she receives a commission, which is payment for having successfully completed the transaction. In the same way, a brokerage house charges a commission for facilitating a futures transaction. In futures trading, however, a transaction is not considered final until the trader's initial position has been closed. Therefore, a commission is not charged when a trader first enters the market, no matter whether the initial position is long or short. When that position is offset, or liquidated, a commission is then charged. A commodity broker's commission, then, represents payment for two transactions: getting into the market and getting out of the market. This is called, appropriately enough, a *round turn,* or a *round trip.* Thus, broker's commissions are usually quoted at a price per round turn.

As we noted earlier, the amount of commission paid will vary depending upon the service expected or rendered. Prices may vary from $15 or $20 for a no-frills discount broker to $125 or more for a full-service broker.

## DAY TRADING VERSUS POSITION TRADING

A position commodity trader initiates a position in the market with the intention of holding that position for more than a short time period—a few days, a week, several weeks. Position trading is designed to profit from longer-term price trends by getting in at a price and waiting for the market to move far enough to provide substantial profits.

There was a time when virtually all futures traders were position traders, except those actually trading on the floor of the exchange. Prior to the availability of sophisticated real-time electronic quote equipment, a trader had to rely on either the newspaper or a broker for price information. The newspaper, of course, provides only the daily price range and the closing price, and brokers could not provide up-to-the-minute price information quickly enough to allow short-term trades to be made with confidence.

In the last decade, however, a plethora of electronic equipment has come on the market at prices that make very sophisticated quote equipment available and affordable for the serious trader. By purchasing a personal computer, some software, the necessary equipment for reception, and paying the required exchange fees, an individual can receive tick-by-tick price information as trading is being conducted. This makes it possible to day trade from home with confidence in the price information being used. As a consequence, day trading has become popular with a large group of traders who attempt to extract profits from the price moves that occur during the course of a trading day.

Most of the techniques for day trading are very similar to position trading—developing charts, trend lines, moving averages, and so forth—with the exception that the time periods used are much shorter—30-minute or 60-minute periods versus daily charts. And with the software currently available, the day trader need never keep a chart by hand again. There are systems that will run any of dozens of technical analyses on historical data as well as on current price data. There are also professional developed trading systems that will provide real-time buy-sell signals to the day trader.

Anyone wishing to day trade in today's highly volatile futures markets, however, should do so with caution. Intraday trading requires a major commitment of time and concentration. A half-hearted attempt will almost certainly result in failure. Day trading can get expensive, with the investment in equipment and exchange subscription fees for price quotes, as well as commission fees on a large number of trades. In spite of the expense and the risk, however, a growing number of futures traders are choosing to day trade rather than to trade longer-term positions.

A number of brokerage firms are responding to this trend by opening up trading rooms for customers to use. Thus, the trader who wants to day trade but who wishes to avoid the expense of all the equipment and fees can now go to a broker's office, where a room has been outfitted with quote equipment and other facilities to allow day trading.

## HEDGING

The basic purpose for the existence of futures trading is the transfer of risk from producers and users of a commodity to speculators (futures traders). When a business person uses the futures market to protect against adverse price movements, the process is called hedging.

Hedging involves taking a position in the futures market that is opposite to the position held in the cash or spot market. In other words, if a business person owns or buys a commodity in the cash market, he or she would then hedge that position by selling an equivalent quantity in the futures market. This selling hedge locks in a price for that inventory while it is being held. If prices go down during the time the commodity is being held, the holder of the commodity loses money in the cash market. This loss, however, is covered by an equivalent price drop in the futures market where, by virtue of being a seller, the business person will show a profit. This profit offsets the loss in the cash market and maintains the net price to the holder at a level very close to the original value of the commodity.

Likewise, if the price of the commodity rises, the holder will show a profit in the cash market and an offsetting loss in the futures market, maintaining the value of the inventory at a constant net value.

The buying hedge is used by a business person who anticipates buying a commodity at a future date and wishes to protect himself or herself from a possible price increase. This person is said to be short the cash market (he or she is "short" of the commodity at the present time) and so would take a long position in the futures market (be a buyer). If prices do go up, this person will have to pay more for the commodity but at the same time will make an equivalent amount in the futures market, thus offsetting the loss in the cash market. If prices decline, the commodity can be bought more cheaply in the cash market, but this advantage is offset by a loss in the futures market.

Hedging, then, not only protects against the possible losses of adverse price movement, it also takes away the possibility of windfall profits that can accrue as the result of favorable price moves. To the cautious business person, however, such potential profits represent too great a risk and are best transferred to the speculator.

In theory hedging provides ideal price protection to the business person, but in practice this protection may be less than ideal. A number of factors can affect the net value of the hedge, and they often do.

When we began our discussion of hedging, we assumed that cash prices and futures prices would move together exactly the same. In practice, this rarely occurs. Conditions in the spot market can pressure prices up or down while not affecting the more distant futures months. Also, local conditions can affect the local cash price while the futures price, which reflects national and international conditions, is unaffected. This difference between the futures price and the spot price is known as the *basis.* For a hedge to work perfectly, the basis must remain constant to the end of the hedge. Thus, if the difference between spot corn and December corn futures is two cents when the hedge is put on, the basis must also be two cents when the hedge is lifted and the corn is sold, if the hedge is to work perfectly.

In fact, the basis will likely change, and this change in the basis will result in either fewer profits or more profits for the hedger. If the local spot price of corn, for example, declines 20 cents by the time it is sold, but the futures price declines only 15 cents, then five cents per bushel was left unprotected, as the basis changed by five cents. Table 6-1 demonstrates what happened.

Various factors can cause a differential between cash and futures prices. First, there are many grades of each commodity traded on the cash market, and each grade changes price at a different rate. A futures contract, however, is limited to one specified grade. It may be that the price of the grade being hedged moves more quickly on the spot market than the grade covered by the futures contract. Second, local cash prices may reflect local market conditions that do not affect futures prices, which are indicative of national and international conditions. Third, more distant futures months are less affected by current market conditions than are spot prices. Fourth,

TABLE 6-1. BASE EXAMPLE.

| Date | Cash | March Futures | Basis |
|------|------|---------------|-------|
| November | $5.30/bushel | $5.47/bushel | $-0.07 |
| February | $5.10/bushel | $5.22/bushel | $-0.12 |
| Gain/Loss | $-0.20 | $-0.15 | $-0.50 |

the commodity being hedged may not be exactly the same as the commodity covered by the futures contract. A clothing manufacturer, for example, may want to hedge the price of yarn in the cotton futures market, but the price of yarn, because it reflects other manufacturing costs as well as the price of cotton, may not fluctuate exactly with cotton prices.

A further limitation of hedging is that the futures contract covers a specified quantity, which may be different from the size of the inventory being hedged. If a farmer expects to sell 18,000 bushels of corn, for example, he or she would only be able to hedge 15,000 bushels by selling three contracts of corn. The remaining 3,000 bushels are unprotected. If the farmer decided to sell four contracts, the additional 2,000 bushels would be a speculative investment. Either way, there is some risk left untransferred.

Hedging, then, covers only major risk factors for individuals and companies engaged in various business ventures. It does not provide complete insurance, but it does significantly reduce the price risks associated with doing business. Hedging is essentially the exchange of one kind of risk, price fluctuation, for another, basis fluctuation.

## *SPREADS AND STRADDLES*

Just as there is often a differential between the cash price and the futures price of a commodity, so is there often a difference in the price fluctuations of various contract months of the same commodity or in the fluctuation of price of one commodity traded on different exchanges. This price differential can result from any number of circumstances.

In a normal market, the price of the spot month, or the contract month closest to delivery, is usually quite close to the cash price of the same commodity, even though, as we have seen, there may be some variance. This phenomenon is easy to explain and is a logical consequence of the fact that a futures contract can be held to delivery.

If the price differential between a futures contract at expiration and the spot price of the same commodity were significant, a trader could easily make money by moving between the two markets. If, for example, the futures price of corn at expiration is 10 cents higher than the cash price, a speculator could simply sell corn on the futures market, buy corn on the cash market, and make delivery of the cash corn to fulfill the futures contract obligation. The result would be a risk-free profit of 10 cents per bushel, less commissions and transaction fees. Likewise, if the futures price is 10 cents lower, a speculator can buy on the futures market, take delivery, then resell on the cash market for a 10-cent profit. Dealing with the cash market is not as difficult as it sounds. Usually, it involves simply the exchange of warehouse receipts.

In a normal market, also, the price of each succeeding contract month after the spot month is higher than the price of the contract immediately preceding it. This normal price increase, called a *premium,* represents the carrying charges involved in holding a commodity in inventory—charges such as storage fees, interest on the capital invested in the commodity, and insurance against loss. Thus, a normal market is also commonly referred to as a carrying-charge market.

Sometimes, however, a market becomes inverted, or backward, and the price of each successive contract month is lower, rather than higher. They are said to be at a discount to the front month. This usually results from buying pressure on the cash market, which drives prices up and thereby encourages those who are holding the commodity in storage to sell rather than to hold. This situation is also known as a *short squeeze* and can result either from normal market conditions (e.g., a temporary shortage) or an attempt by some individual or group of individuals to corner the market by buying all available supplies, thus driving prices up artificially and putting the squeeze on those who must purchase the commodity (the shorts). These kinds of market conditions can provide opportunities for lower-risk profits to the astute spread trader, although spread trading is not necessarily less risky than trading outright positions.

A *spread* is simply the simultaneous buying of one contract and selling of another. To be a true spread, however, there must be some reason to believe that the conditions that will cause price movement in one contract will also cause price movement in the other.

There are three types of spreads. First, there is the *intra-market spread,* where positions are taken in two contract months of the same commodity. If a trader notes, for example, that the price differential between May corn and July corn exceeds normal carrying charges (July is at a premium to May), he or she might buy a contract of May corn and sell a contract of July corn. Later, as the differential narrows, to bring the July corn contract more into line with normal costs, the trader will see a profit on the change in the difference. The intra-market spread trader is not concerned with the absolute price of a commodity, only the changes that occur in the premium or discount.

The second type of spread is known as the *inter-commodity spread.* As the name implies, this is a spread between two different commodities—buying one and selling the other. Again, to be a true spread, there must be some relationship between the two commodities that will tend to cause the prices to move in the same direction simultaneously. If not, the spread becomes a dangerously risky trade, as the two positions can easily move in opposite directions, incurring losses on both trades. Such movement, of course, defeats the purpose of spread trading. In a typical spread, one of the trades will show a loss while the other will show a profit. The profit to the trader occurs when the relative difference between the two prices (the premium or discount) changes in a favorable direction.

In certain markets, there are relationships between commodities that will allow true spread trading. Among the grains, for example, corn may become a substitute for beans as a feed if the price of beans gets too high and vice versa. Thus, the prices will tend to move together. Another common inter-commodity spread is the *crush spread,* which is a trade involving soybeans and its two derivatives, soybean meal and soybean oil. When the beans are crushed, they produce meal and oil. In all such inter-commodity spreads, there is a natural relationship that tends to limit the magnitude of the price differential between the commodities. To profit from such a relationship, however, the spread trader must know the history and the characteristics of the relationship.

A third possible spread relationship exists when one commodity is traded on different exchanges, such as Kansas City wheat, CBOT wheat, and Minneapolis wheat. This is known as an *inter-market spread.* Whenever the price difference for a commodity between two exchanges exceeds the normal cost of transporting the commodity from one delivery point to the other, there is every reason to believe that the differential will narrow at some time in the future to reflect the true delivery cost. If wheat is selling at a significantly higher price in Chicago than in Kansas City, for example, merchants would buy the wheat in Kansas City and ship the wheat to Chicago to sell it, if the price difference exceeded the transportation costs.

Also, producers would ship to Chicago rather than Kansas City to sell their wheat if the price there would pay all shipping charges and still show a higher return. This relationship tends to limit the difference in prices that can occur among the various exchanges and thus presents a potential spread opportunity any time the price differential exceeds transportation costs between two exchanges.

*Trading Spreads*

As noted in my book titled *How to Profit from Seasonal Commodity Spreads. A Complete Guide* (Wiley, New York, 1983), commodity traders often ignore the spread as a speculative vehicle, considering it more the domain of professional commercial interests. Spreads, however, offer greater potential for profit and higher reliability than net positions in the futures markets, particularly when the seasonal or cyclic tendencies of spreads are studied and used advantageously.

There are those who say that spread trading also involves less risk than trading in net positions, but this is a gross misstatement of the facts. Although there are some seasonal commodity spreads that are inherently less risky than certain net market positions, there are other extremely high-risk spreads at the opposite end of the continuum. As with all futures trading, spread trading remains a high-risk, high-reward venture.

Profits in spread trading are made in one of three ways: (1) the short position makes more money than the long position loses during the period of time the contracts are held; (2) the long position makes more money than the short position loses during the time the contracts are held; (3) both positions make money. Losses occur in just the opposite fashion: (1) the short position loses more money than the long position makes; (2) the long position loses more than the short position makes; (3) both positions lose money.

Another name for a commodity spread is *straddle,* which states in a more concise fashion the exact nature of a spread. With a spread, the trader is effectively straddling the market, very much like a rider straddles a horse: with one leg on each side of the saddle. In fact, a popular phrase in commodity trading is "lifting one leg" of a spread, which refers to the action of exiting one position while leaving the other position on, thereby remaining net long or net short, depending on which side of the spread, or straddle, was exited.

### Margin Requirements with Spreads

Exchange margins for certain recognized spreads are generally lower than the margin required for net futures positions. This reflects the exchange's belief that a spread is generally less risky than a net position, because the potential losses in one position are at least partially covered by the potential gains in the other. Certainly, in an ideal spread situation, as prices of one leg of the spread change, the prices of the other change at nearly the same rate and in the same direction, so that the losses incurred by one side are offset by the gains in the other while the premium or discount changes advantageously in order to provide profits to the trader.

Such low margin requirements, however, can lure a trader into a false sense of security. For one thing, as with all futures trading, the trade might move disadvantageously before it makes the right move. A trader who has met only the minimum margin requirements might find that such a move necessitates a margin call or, worse yet, a forced liquidation of both positions at a loss. A good strategy to avoid such a circumstance is to maintain at least twice the minimum margin in the trading account in order to provide plenty of leeway for each position.

### Commissions on Spreads

Spread trading is by its nature often a low-profit trade. Because profits accrue not from the magnitude of the price move in the market but from the change in the difference in prices between two positions, the potential for large profits on any one trade is small. Many spread trades accrue profits of only $200 to $300. If the brokerage fee is $65 to $125, the net profit from the trade is obviously quite small.

Therefore, it is probably better for a spread trader to do his or her own market research and then utilize the services of a discount broker, who will charge considerably less commission. To aid in this research, there are several good books and advisory services available.

*Market Research and Study*

The fact is that, with some quality assistance from one or more good sources, spread trading is probably a better strategy for the part-time trader who has little time to watch the markets than is net position trading, because the research necessary to locate good potential spread trades is somewhat easier than the technical or fundamental analysis necessary to trade net positions successfully. This does not mean that profits are any easier to come by—they're not. The education and preparation necessary for effective spread trading is just as critical as with all futures trading. But with the market information available to the average part-time trader, who depends on the newspaper and a broker for price information, spread trading may be easier to do profitably.

Still, maintaining current information on all the potential spreads is probably unrealistic for most part-time traders, or full-time traders for that matter, unless they have a computer system that can regularly update charts. One solution is to subscribe to a spread chart service, such as *Spreadscope*, P.O. Box 5841, Mission Hills, California 91345. This kind of service can be very helpful, particularly since spread trading usually requires only weekly charting rather than the daily or shorter-term charts required by net futures trading.

*Market Entry and Exit*

The most difficult part of any trading, whether spread or net position, is actual market entry. Charts and calculations may indicate substantial profits to be made by various spread strategies, but unless the spread is entered at the right price, it might turn out to be a low-profit or even a losing trade, no matter how good it looks on paper. Market entry, however, is a chore that requires both skill and a touch of artistry. For many reasons, both psychological and technical, order placement is perhaps the greatest obstacle standing in the way of successful trading. The time that elapses from a signal to actual market entry can be critical. Thus, a successful spread trader must know the various entry and exit orders available for spreads and the advantages and disadvantages of each. The following presentation and analysis of spread orders is taken from *How to Profit from Seasonal Commodity Spreads. A Complete Guide* (Wiley, New York, 1983).

*1. Entry at the market.* The most certain way to establish a spread or net position is to enter at the market. Although this procedure may not cause problems in most net positions, it can account for especially poor price fills in spreads. In order to appreciate how spread price fills can be especially poor when done at the market, it is important to understand how the floor trader executing a spread order fulfills his obligation. Since most pit brokers (floor traders) are extremely busy and since they cannot be in two places in the pit at once, it is not incumbent upon them to shop around for the best possible spread price. If an order is given to them at the market and market volume is especially thin (low), they will simply execute at the going price. When the market is thinly traded, the going price on the long side will be higher than expected, and the going price on the short side will be lower than expected. Hence, a trader can come out behind in two ways. Instead of getting just one poor price fill, as in a net position, he or she will end up with two poor price fills at a spread differential that is usually not close to that expected. The thinner the market the more likely a poor fill. Whether entering or exiting a market, a trader should use market orders as a last choice, a desperation order, something I call an LMO (Let Me Out).

The only advantage of a market order is that it guarantees a position no matter what. There are a few conditions, however, under which a market order would be advisable. If, for example, an ideal opportunity to enter or to exit a given spread has been missed, a market order might be justified. If a stop point has been penetrated and it is important to exit the market immediately, a market order is justified. If a spread position has been carried into the delivery period and it is absolutely necessary to liquidate in order to avoid delivery, a market order is justified. In any event, the rule of thumb is that entry at the market or exit at the market almost always guarantees a poor price fill, so a trader shouldn't be surprised; it's certainly not the broker's fault.

2. *Legging in and legging out.* A common but not necessarily wise procedure for spread entry and exit is the legging in and legging out procedure. As the term implies, this technique involves entering a spread one side, or leg, at a time or exiting a spread one side, or leg, at a time. Typically, a spread is legged in or out by traders who have been carrying a net position that went against them and who then spread the position up in order to avoid further loss. Hence, they have legged into a spread many times with good reason, and when it comes time to close out one side of a spread, they leg out. This is a technique that cannot only complicate matters but also can increase the risk of losses.

3. *Spread entry on price orders.* The method of entering spreads that makes the most sense is entering on a price order. In other words, an order is placed with the broker to establish a spread at a specific premium or discount. The advantage of this technique is, of course, that a spread will not be entered at a price different from that which was expected. The single great disadvantage is that the order may not get filled. If the order is placed at too ambitious an entry price (the trader is trying to save money) while the trader is expecting the market to come to that price, the entire move can be missed. On the other hand, entering the market may cause the trader to lose a good percentage of the potential profit simply in poor order fills. Order placement at specific prices is as much an art as it is a science.

## Spreads as an Index to Market Behavior

Spreads can be most helpful in determining the validity of net market trends, even when the spreads are not traded themselves. Most spreads tend to divide themselves into bull or bear categories quite readily. Thus, in a typical bull market, the nearby contract month is likely to gain over the deferred contract month. Conversely, a bear spread and a bear market go hand in hand wherein the nearby contract month tends to lose to the distant contract month, a situation that tends to continue throughout the span of the bear trend. Thus, market technicians and fundamentalists alike will use spread behavior as an index to the present and future direction of the markets. The assumption is that the majority of traders interested in spreads are professionals, and when these professionals, for example, begin accumulating nearby months while selling the distant months, their behavior is based on extensive fundamental knowledge of the markets and is reflected in the changing spread relationship.

### Sample Spread Charts

The charts that accompany this section on spread trading offer some very good examples of spread relationships. The first chart (Figure 6-1) shows one in which the long leg made more profit than the short leg loss; in other words, the chart shows the spread differential as it moves higher. The scale at left is not a price scale per se but rather a price difference scale. As long as the scale remains in positive territory, it is an indication that the long contract month is gaining over the short contract month.

Figure 6-2 shows the opposite situation. The scale at left indicates that the spread is trading in minus territory, which means that the short contract month is trading at a higher price than the long contract month in this period. In other words, the deferred contract month is at a premium to the nearby contract month, whereas in the previous situation the nearby contract month was trading at a premium to the deferred contract month. In this case, money will be made on the spread if one is short the nearby contract month and long the distant contract month.

Figures 6-3 and 6-4 show the same basic relationship in commodity spreads but in different markets— the very popular wheat/corn and pork belly/live hog spreads.

## FUTURES OPTIONS TRADING

The newcomer to the world of futures trading is the *futures option,* which adds an entirely new dimension to the industry. Although the concept of trading futures options may initially seem confusing, it is really quite easy to understand if an individual already has a basic understanding of what a futures contract really is.

Forget for a moment that an option on a futures contract is twice removed from the underlying commodity. Think instead of what an option really is. An option simply offers the buyer the choice of whether to take a futures position or not. In other words, a futures option gives the buyer of the option the right to buy or sell the underlying futures contract at a given price at some time in the future, regardless of what the actual price may be at that time. The beauty of such an instrument is readily apparent. Once a speculator owns an option to buy or sell at an established price, he or she may then exercise that option if it becomes profitable to do so or not exercise it if it does not become profitable to do so. The decision as to whether or not to exercise the option provides a riskless choice: enter if there is a profit, stay out if there is not.

Historically, futures options have not enjoyed a particularly virtuous reputation. In the 1860s, the Chicago Board of Trade established a prohibition on options trading, as a result of various abuses of the practice, a ruling

*Figure 6-1.*

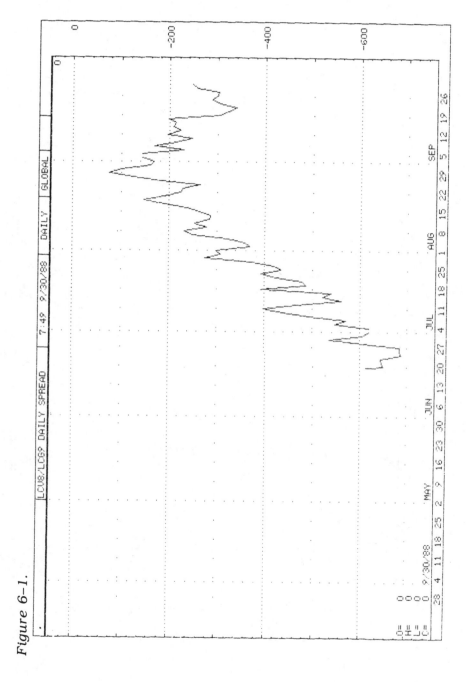

*Figure 6-2.*

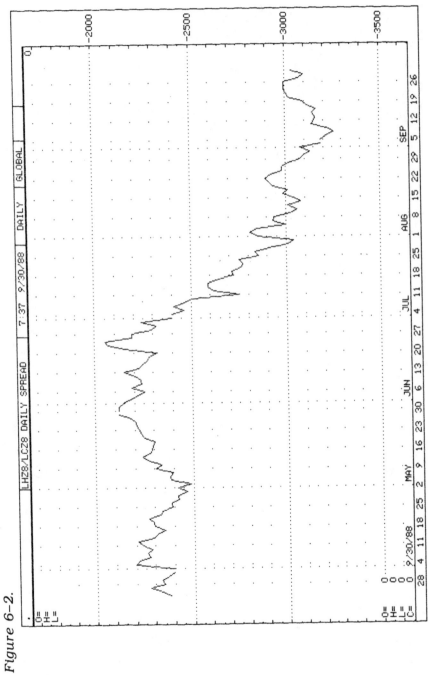

*Figure 6-3.*

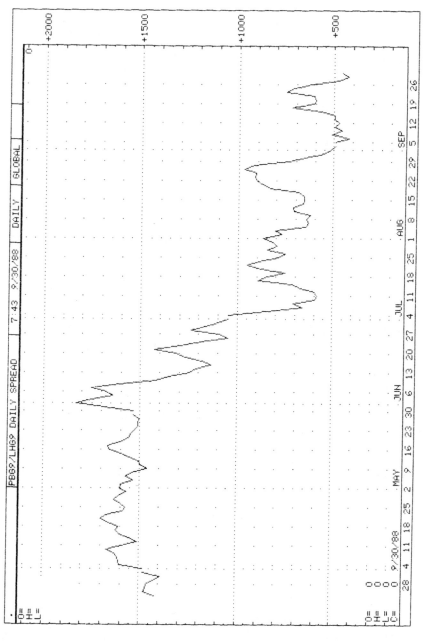

*Figure 6–4.*

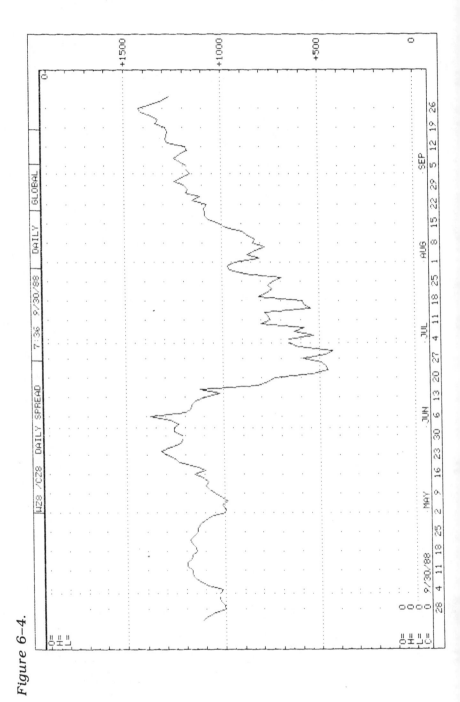

that was reversed a few years later when a new board of governors assumed control. Futures options trading has since occurred intermittently, as supporters of options trading have often squared off against those opposed. The long-running battle has included both lawsuits and legislation, as partisans on both sides have waged an intense war around the issue. Only recently has futures options trading become sufficiently regulated and standardized to attempt to take a recognized position next to futures trading as a legitimate and respected economic instrument.

Unfortunately, much of the tarnished reputation of futures options has been earned. In 1936 options traders were implicated in a successful attempt to manipulate the markets at the CBOT. Throughout the 1930s, unregulated options trading was occurring both at the exchanges and off the floor of the exchanges. These option "privileges" generally had expiration dates that were only one to seven days removed, giving them the image of gambling and making them virtually useless to commercial interests that wished to shift longer-term risk. These options were subsequently banned by the Commodity Exchange Act. Then, during the early 1970s, several unscrupulous firms began selling London commodity options to unwary American speculators at extremely high markups while charging huge commissions. As a result, Congress considered banning the trading of all commodity options during the 1974 hearings but changed its mind after hearing testimony from many sources in support of the economic benefits of commodity options trading. Since 1982, futures options trading has been allowed on organized U.S. exchanges under the watchful eye of the Commodity Futures Trading Commission.

One of the difficulties in trading in futures options is that an entirely new vocabulary is required if a trader is to get involved. The most important thing to remember is that there are two kinds of options: a *put option* and a *call option*. As the names suggest, a put option conveys the right to sell the underlying option whereas a call option conveys the right to buy the underlying option. Either a put or a call option can be bought or sold, but buying one does not offset the purchase of the other. That is, the only way to offset an options position is to complete the opposite transaction with the same option: If a put option is bought, that same put option must be sold before the trader is out of the market.

Every option has a limited lifetime and is scheduled to expire at some specified time just prior to the scheduled delivery month of the underlying futures contract. This *expiration date* is set by the exchange.

The strike price, or *exercise price,* of the option is the price at which the buyer of the option may buy (with a call) or sell (with a put) the underlying commodity. The options trader does not have an unlimited choice of strike prices. Usually, the available strike prices for a particular option are listed by the exchange in standardized increments. The buyer must choose one of those standardized strike prices when buying the option.

To review the vocabulary so far, a put provides the right to sell the underlying commodity and a call provides the right to buy. The expiration date is the last day on which the option may be exercised. It is standardized and established by the exchange. The strike price, or exercise price, is the price at which the underlying commodity may be bought (call) or sold (put).

In trading commodity futures options, there is always a buyer and a seller of the option. The buyer, as we have seen, buys the right (but not an obligation) to buy or sell the underlying commodity at a preestablished price (the strike price). The seller of the option (also known as the *option writer*) sells the option to the buyer. If the option buyer chooses to exercise the option, the seller of the option is obligated to take the opposite side of the underlying futures contract.

If, for example, an options trader buys a put (the right to sell) for November soybeans at a strike price of $7 per bushel and three weeks later chooses to exercise the option when the price of soybeans goes to $6.50 per bushel, the seller of the option must then take the long position in the futures contract. In this situation, the option buyer, by going short at $7 (the option strike price) can offset that position by buying soybeans at $6.50 (the present market price), thus showing a profit of $0.50 per bushel, minus the cost of the option and the broker's commission. The seller of the option, however, has lost money on the futures transaction. Because he or she is a buyer of soybeans at $7 (the option strike price) and a seller at $6.50 (the market price), the loss is $0.50 per bushel. To offset part of that loss, however, the option seller has received payment for the option from the option buyer in the form of a premium.

Most options, however, are not exercised. Rather, they are traded much like they were a commodity themselves. Therefore, instead of exercising the option when soybeans went to $6.50, as in the previous example, the option buyer would likely sell the option at that point, at a price that would reflect the additional value of the option. Who would buy the put option? Someone who thought the price of soybeans would go even lower.

In this example, it can readily be seen that the buyer of an option incurs a very limited risk—the cost of the option plus the broker's commission—while the option seller incurs unlimited risk—the same risk as a futures trader. Why would anyone become an option writer if the risk is so great? Certainly, the novice options trader should stay away from writing options. Many experienced traders, however, will include option writing as part of an overall trading strategy.

Sometimes a trader will write an option while holding the opposite position in the futures market. This is called *covered option* writing. For example, a trader might buy one live cattle futures contact while selling one live cattle call. If the buyer of the call exercises the option, the option seller will be obligated to sell a live cattle future at the strike price. This futures position, however, is covered by the long position previously taken, thus limiting the risk associated with writing the call. An option not covered in this manner is called a *naked option* and obviously is a very risky maneuver.

When a trader buys an option, the price paid is called the premium. The amount of the premium is determined by supply and demand and the market forces in the pit. There are, however, several factors that contribute to the value of the option.

The most obvious factor is the price of the underlying future. This is called the intrinsic value of the option. If, as in our previous example, soybeans are trading at $6.50, a $7 put has an intrinsic value of $0.50 times 5,000 bushels, equaling $2,500. If, however, soybeans are trading at $7.50, a $7 put has no intrinsic value. It is said to be out of the money. At $6.50, a $7 put is in the money. An in-the-money option, therefore, has intrinsic value equal to the difference between the strike price and the current market price of the future. An out-of-the-money option has no intrinsic value.

A second factor that adds value to an option is time. The further an option is from its expiration date, the greater the possibility that the market might move in the right direction and thus increase the intrinsic value of the option. Therefore, an out-of-the-money option with 60 days to expiration is worth more than an out-of-the-money option with only 15 days to expiration.

A third factor contributing to the value of an option is the volatility of the market. The more volatile the market, the more an option buyer is willing to pay for an option in order to alleviate some of that risk. Conversely, an option writer must charge a higher premium to offset the greater risk taken by writing an option in a volatile market.

There are numerous computer programs available that will help a trader figure the value of an option. In addition, many options traders use their own rule-of-thumb formulas to arrive at an approximate value of a given option. Anyone seriously interested in trading options would be well-advised to read one or more of the many excellent books on options trading now on the market.

### Margin in Options Trading

For an option buyer, there is no margin cost per se. There is only the cost of the premium plus commission costs. To many novice traders, this characteristic of options trading is very attractive. They can go to sleep at night without worrying whether they might receive a margin call in the morning. An option seller, however, must post margin exactly as if he or she were trading a futures contract. The reason is clear: If the option buyer elects to exercise the option, the option writer immediately has a futures position and probably at a loss, since the buyer would not likely exercise unless there was a profit to be made.

### Exit Alternatives

The option seller, or writer, has no discretionary choices available once the option is sold and the premium has been received. From that point on, all of the decision-making power lies with the buyer, who has three choices. First, the buyer of an option can simply allow the option to expire worthless. This alternative would be chosen if the option remained out-of-the-money and therefore never attained any intrinsic value.

A second alternative is to offset the option by selling an identical option, just as one would do in a futures contract. Remember, however, that to offset an option, the identical option must be sold. A put does not offset a call or vice versa. Likewise, selling an option at a different strike price does not offset the original option. The only way to offset an option that has been purchased is to sell an identical option at the same strike price.

The third alternative available to an option buyer is to exercise the option. This alternative would be chosen if, as in the soybean example, the option is far enough in the money that its intrinsic value exceeds the original cost of the premium and commission. The strategy would be to exercise the option, then offset the futures position, and take the profits.

*Advantages of Options Trading*

Trading in options offers several advantages to trading in the underlying futures. The most popular and popularized advantage, of course, is that an option has limited and known risk. The option buyer risks only the cost of premium plus commission. The worst that can happen is that the option expires worthless and the entire original investment is lost. But there is never a margin call.

A second advantage that options trading offers is leverage. It is possible to buy an out-of-the-money option with 60 days to expiration for $300 to $800. If the market makes a fairly good move during that 60 days, the option can provide profits of several thousand dollars.

A third advantage to options trading is staying power. If a trader is convinced that a certain market is due for a major bull market move, he or she might buy a call rather than taking a long futures position, with the idea that if, in the short term, the market goes lower before embarking on its run up, there will not be the risk of excessive margin calls or, worse yet, the necessity to get out of the market at a loss because of dwindling capital.

For hedgers, options are particularly attractive because, especially in a volatile market, they can preserve needed capital if prices move too far in the wrong direction. If a futures position is held as a hedge, an adverse move can result in substantial margin calls, thereby tying up additional capital. With an option, however, only the original cost of the premium is invested.

*Disadvantages of Options Trading*

Naturally, any speculative venture that can be packaged and sold as attractively as can options must have a down side, and options certainly do. All of those brokers who extoll options as a wonderful investment because of their limited risk factor neglect to mention that it is just as hard, if not harder, to make money in options trading as it is in futures trading. Although the loss exposure is limited and known, a loss is still a loss, and several limited losses in a row add up to a large loss. Limited risk doesn't mean the trader can't lose money— only that he or she knows up front how much can be lost. Profitable options trading, as with all futures trading, requires strategy and discipline. The risk with options, however, is that a trader can be lulled into a false sense of security and therefore neglect to keep a watchful eye on the market.

Another concern with buying options is that, to show profits, prices must move far enough to cover first the cost of the premium. Thus, many small price changes that would have been profitable to a futures trader can turn out to be unprofitable to an option buyer. In soybeans, for example, if a trader buys a put option at a strike price of $6.50 and pays $460 premium plus 20% commission ($92) when beans are trading for $7, the price of beans would have to fall below $6.39 before any profit would be made. (A one-cent move in soybeans is $50. The cost of premium plus commission is $552.00. If beans fall 11 cents below $6.50, the strike price, the option would show sufficient intrinsic value to cover most of that cost). Had a trader simply sold short at $7, the same move would have netted $3,050 minus commissions.

A final disadvantage to options trading is the high cost of commissions. Because options traders are usually taking a long-term position, the volume of trading in an individual account is not high, causing brokers to charge higher commission rates for option trades. Some brokers charge unwary clients as high as 40% of the premium as a commission. On a $2,000 premium, that amounts to $800 in commission costs. Other brokers will charge only their standard commission fee. Anyone wishing to trade options, therefore, would be well advised to shop around for a broker who provides the desired level of service at a reasonable commission rate. Otherwise, the only one making money might be the options broker.

### Strategies for Trading Options

Options trading offers a plethora of trading strategies ranging from the most elementary to some that are quite esoteric and sophisticated. The reader is cautioned to consult a more thorough text on options trading before attempting any sophisticated trades. Nevertheless, some of the more popular strategies are presented here as an example of what can be done with options alone or with options and futures together.

*Strategy #1: Long call.* Buy a call option rather than going long. Although this strategy seems simple enough, even a plan this elementary requires some decision making and some rudimentary knowledge of the market. If a trader expects a short-term move, he or she might buy an in-the-money option or one that is near the money. Although they cost more, such options will move at the same rate or faster than the underlying future. Alternatively, a trader might buy an option further from the money by virtue of its nearer expiration or larger distance from the strike price. Although such options may cost less, they may move only one-third as quickly as the underlying contract. This ratio between the price move of the futures and the price move of the option is known as the *delta*. A futures contract has a delta of one: Each time the price moves one cent, the value of the contract position moves one cent. An option with a delta of 0.33 moves approximately one-third as fast as the underlying contract. To make informed decisions about the best strategy to pursue, in even a plan as simple as this, it is wise to use an options evaluation program.

*Strategy #2: Long put.* Buy a put option rather than selling short. As with the first strategy, several alternatives are available for an expected short-term move or a longer-term move.

*Strategy #3: Synthetic long call.* Use a put option to protect a long futures position. To an extent, this is a spread strategy. If the market shows an extended rise in price, the futures position will show significant profits, and the cost of the protection is limited to the options premium plus commission. If prices fall, however, the option will increase in value as the futures contract declines, although not necessarily on a par. Remember that time decay is also a factor in the value of an option.

*Strategy #4: Synthetic long put.* Sell short the futures while buying a call for protection. The opposite of strategy #3, this works very similarly to buying a put, and it requires the right combination of strike price and expiration to provide protection.

*Strategy #5: Long straddle.* If a major move is expected, but the direction is impossible to predict, buy both a put and a call. With this plan, the only way to suffer a loss is if the market fails to make the expected move during the life span of the two options.

*Strategy #6: Covered option.* Sell a call or a put, but cover the position with the opposite futures position. If a call is sold, cover with a short futures position. If a put is sold, cover with a long futures position.

*Strategy #7: Butterfly spread.* Buy a nearby option, buy a deferred option, and sell two mid-term options for a long butterfly. Sell the ends and buy the middle for a short butterfly. This spread strategy can combine exceptionally low risk with tremendous profit potential, if the timing is correct and the market has been conceptualized accurately. To work, there must be a differential in long-, short-, and intermediate-term movements. This set of circumstances can occur quite easily in the interest rate market when short-term rates decline while long-term rates hold steady or when long-term rates decline while short-term rates go up.

*Strategy #8: Short straddle.* Sell both a put and a call. Used when volatility is declining, this allows a trader to collect both premiums. Maximum profit is earned if the options expire while the futures price and the strike price are the same.

*Strategy #9: Long strangle.* Buy a put and a call that have different strike prices but a common expiration date. Similar to a straddle, which consists of options with the same strike price and expiration date, the purpose of a strangle is the same: to be positioned when a major breakout occurs.

*Strategy #10: Short strangle.* Sell a put and a call with different strike price and a common expiration date. Like a short straddle, this strategy is designed to profit from markets with low volatility. This position creates unlimited risk, however.


## REGULATORY AGENCIES

Through the centuries, the practice of futures trading has always been somewhat suspect. After all, how can someone sell what he does not own? In the original Japanese Dojima Rice Market, the government temporarily halted trading in the 17th century because of irregularities, as well as the fact that, with no cash settlement being allowed, futures trading was little more than gambling.

As commodity futures trading became more popular in the United States, various attempts were made to regulate the process and to control various manipulative and fraudulent practices. Because the futures market is in many ways the essence of a free market capitalist economy, attempts to regulate and restrict the business have met with solid resistance through the years. The balance has always been between protecting the unwary from unscrupulous tactics and placing undo restrictions on a free market economy.

The earliest government regulation of futures trading in the United States occurred in 1916 with enactment of the Cotton Futures Act. This was followed in 1922 with the Grain Futures Act, which was amended in the 1930s and changed to the Commodity Exchange Act. With this act, administered by a division of the Department of Agriculture called the Commodity Exchange Authority, the government outlawed some of the most blatant manipulative practices and established rules whereby customers' money would be kept safe from unscrupulous brokers.

In 1974 Congress passed the Commodity Futures Trading Commission Act, which established governmental authority over all commodities, rights, and services traded on futures contracts. The Commodity Futures Trading Commission (CFTC) was established with two goals in mind: (1) to foster competition and (2) to protect the participants in the futures markets from fraud, deceit, and abusive practices. To accomplish these goals, the CFTC requires that every person involved with the execution of orders or in dealing with the public be registered. Registration involves demonstration of a basic understanding of the business through standardized testing and a personal record that is clear of involvement in illegal or unethical practices. For this purpose, fingerprinting is a required part of the registration procedure.

The CFTC has established a number of specific categories of individuals in the futures business, each with its own set of requirements and regulations. These include the Introducing Broker (IB), who introduces business through a Futures Commission Merchant (FCM), who may or may not be a clearing member of an exchange. Other categories include the Commodity Trading Advisor (CTA), the Commodity Pool Operator (CPO), and the Associated Person (AP) working for any of the above persons.

## National Futures Association

The National Futures Association (NFA) is a self-regulatory organization established in 1912 under provisions of the CFTC Act of 1974. Anyone in the futures business who is required to register with the CFTC must also become a member of the NFA.

The primary purpose of the NFA is to assure "high standards of professional conduct and financial responsibility" on the part of its members. To accomplish this, the NFA conducts periodic audits of members' financial records and other records. In addition, the NFA monitors the sales practices of its members, requiring among other things, that certain disclaimers appear on all published documents and that all claims regarding profitability in the futures business be accompanied by statements that describe the risks associated with such investments. The NFA also provides a mechanism for arbitrating disputes arising from futures-related business between NFA members and their customers.

### Who Must Register with the CFTC?

The CFTC is very specific regarding who must register with them. The following descriptions are taken directly from the *National Futures Association Application Guide* for NFA memberships and CFTC registration.

* *Futures Commission Merchant (FCM).* Generally, an FCM is an individual or organization that does both of the following: (1) solicits or accept orders to buy or sell futures contracts or commodity options, and (2) accepts money or other assets from customers to support such orders.

* *Introducing Broker (IB).* An IB is a person or organization that solicits or accepts orders to buy or sell futures contracts or commodity options but does not accept money or other assets from customers to support such orders.

* *Commodity Pool Operator (CPO).* A CPO is an individual or organization that operates or solicits funds for a commodity pool, that is, an enterprise in which funds contributed by a number of persons are combined

for the purpose of trading futures contracts or commodity options.

* *Commodity Trading Advisor (CTA)*. A CTA is a person who, for compensation or profit, directly or indirectly advises others as to the value of or the advisability of buying or selling futures contracts or commodity options. Providing advice indirectly includes exercising trading authority over a customer's account as well as giving advice through written publications or other media.

* *Associated Person (AP)*. An AP is an individual who solicits orders, customers, or customer funds (or who supervises persons so engaged) on behalf of an FCM, IB, CTA, or CPO.

* *Protection for the Individual Investor*. The CFTC seeks to protect the public who are involved in the futures business by establishing extensive regulations, maintaining effective surveillance procedures, and rigidly enforcing the rules. Potential abuses in the futures industry fall into three broad categories: unfair trading practices, credit and financial risks, and sales practice abuses.

Unfair trading practices include price manipulation, prearranged trading, and trading ahead of a customer. The CFTC has stringent surveillance practices in place to detect these abuses.

To guard against the risk of insolvency, the CFTC enforces strict net capital requirements and position limits on firms doing business in the futures industry. Moreover, the CFTC requires that customers' funds be maintained in segregated accounts, separate from the operating capital of the firm.

Sales practices are closely regulated and monitered. Brokers are required to disclose the risk involved in futures trading and are prevented from making wild claims of profitability. Any claim regarding profit must be accompanied by the disclaimer that loss may also occur; any reporting of past profitability must also state that past profits are not necessarily indicative of future profits.

A Commodity Trading Advisor or a Commodity Pool Operator must file a disclosure document with the NFA and include a three-year track record in the disclosure. Brokers are required to know their customers, so that unsuitable recommendations are not made, and are prohibited from furnishing false or misleading information, engaging in high-pressure sales tactics, and employing unqualified or unsupervised sales personnel. Any customer who has experienced fraudulent practices or other illegal activities on the part of a futures broker is entitled to file for money damages under the reparations program operated by the CFTC.

CHAPTER 7

# Fundamental Forces on the Market

At a commodities seminar a few years ago, I had the fortune to meet an individual who seemed to take a keen interest in the soybean market. As he sat down, newspaper in hand, he said to me in an offhand manner, "It rained in Illinois and Indiana last night. The price of beans should be down."

He then turned to the business section, ran his finger down the futures prices until he came to soybeans, and exclaimed, "Yep! Down three cents." With a self-satisfied air, he closed the newspaper and laid it on the floor next to his chair, content with this very simple but correct fundamental analysis of the soybean market. I only wish all analysis of futures markets could be so simple and so accurate!

His basic reasoning, of course, was on target. The growing season had been dry up to that time, leading to predictions of lowered output and thus higher prices. The higher prices would be caused by lowered supply in the face of constant or increased demand. The recent rain would cause increased production, leading to greater supply and hence to lower prices. To the layman, his logic seems faultless. But, believe me, if fundamental analysis of the futures markets were that simple and easy, there would be a lot more wealthy commodity traders running around.

To be a successful fundamental analyst requires careful consideration of a massive amount of information. Just how confusing it can be is captured by this paragraph taken from Perry Kaufman's *The Handbook of Futures Markets* (Wiley, New York, 1986):

> The fundamentalist uses historical economic information to establish a supply-and-demand price curve. He or she then relates estimates of this year's supply-and-demand balance to the historical price to decide if the current price is too high, too low, or just right. To arrive at an estimate of this year's supply, the fundamentalist will examine reports of the number of acres planted of a particular crop. The fundamentalist will also look at the sales of fertilizer and the sales and cost of diesel fuel for farm equipment, in addition to past weather data and predicted weather patterns for both the near- and longer-term periods of the crop's growing season. Information must be taken into account about the productivity of new seeds or strains developed for the crop being considered or for competing crops. The fundamentalist must be aware of the government stockpiles as well as those stockpiled on-farm (visible supply). Government price-support levels and the strength of the dollar will be considered, as it affects exports. The analyst will weigh the cost of interest paid on borrowed money, the impact of competition from substitutes or new products, and will be alert to changes in eating patterns and per capita income affecting de-

mand. This list would have to be extended significantly to include all the primary determinants of price, and yet the accuracy of the current price evaluation depends upon the accuracy of the estimates and the weighting of factors.

Fundamental analysis has its roots in economics. Economic theory is not just one theory; rather, there are many economic theories. Similarly, there are many different approaches to fundamental analysis. The common element of all approaches to fundamental analysis is that they study the purported causes of price increases and price decreases in the hope that they will be able to ascertain changes prior to their occurrences. Their success rests upon the availability of accurate assessments of the variables they analyze, as well as the availability of variables that may not be known to other fundamental analysts.

The plethora of statistics available to the fundamentalist at any given point in time can be overwhelming. The fundamentalist must be selective and prepared to evaluate a massive amount of data. As a consequence, there is no one typical fundamentalist. Rather, there are many different types who evaluate different kinds of data at different times. There are those who, by virtue of their skill and expertise, can provide accurate forecasts, and there are those who, working with the same tools, make worthless forecasts.

## SUPPLY AND DEMAND

The basis of fundamental analysis is supply and demand. But even a concept so simple as that is not without its complications. Basically, a fundamental analyst assumes that anything that decreases supply will tend to raise prices, and anything that increases supply will tend to lower prices. Conversely, increased demand will raise prices, and decreased demand will lower prices.

But now we get into the hard part of supply and demand. To an economist, *demand* for an item means simply how much of a commodity or a service buyers are willing and able to buy at a particular price, at a certain time, in a given place. Normally, there is a close correlation between price and consumption. As price goes up, consumption drops, and vice versa.

However, there are other factors that must be considered when measuring demand. For instance, what is the general state of the economy? During a depression, steak will likely sell more poorly than during prosperity, regardless of lowered prices. Also, what about consumer tastes? In recent years, the American public has become keenly aware of the potentially unhealthful consequences of eating too much red meat. This has resulted in a decline in the demand for beef, independent of price.

A third factor to consider when measuring demand for a product is the availability of alternative products. Consumers may eat steak at lower prices but switch to chicken when the price of steak rises. In the case of wheat, however, there is no readily available substitute for the making of flour for bread, so a simple switch to another product would be less likely during a price increase. Economists measure this tendency to switch by using an index they call *elasticity of demand*. It simply rates a product according to the estimated percentage of consumers who will switch to another product as the price rises.

Just as demand for a product is difficult to measure, *supply* of that product is not always simple to calculate either. As a rule, supply consists of the carryover stocks from the previous marketing year plus the amount being produced this marketing year plus the amount being imported. But, like demand, there is an *elasticity of supply* regarding the price factor. As the price of a commodity rises, more sellers are willing to sell the product, and vice versa. As the price of an agricultural product goes up, for example, more farmers switch to growing that crop. As a consequence, available supply is closely related to price.

Supply is also determined in part by the ability to store the product. The more perishable the commodity, the less likely it can be held off the market in anticipation of better prices. Even with storable commodities, the cost and availability of adequate storage space is an important factor in the determination of supply.

As you can readily see, even the seemingly simple concept of supply and demand becomes very complicated in the process of fundamental analysis of the commodity markets. Fortunately, there are some sources of information that can be helpful.

### Market Reports

The U.S. Department of Agriculture (USDA) provides a number of very thorough and generally accurate reports on daily, weekly, and monthly price movements. The USDA also produces periodic reports estimating ending stocks. These, of course, change during the year as other factors come into play. In addition to government reports, there are private market-reporting services for many commodities, as well as detailed reports published by the exchanges, which provide important statistics on the cash markets.

The analysts who use all this information to make forecasts for the major producers and the large brokerage houses develop an economic model into which they insert the various statistics as they become available. Often, this model is computerized so that voluminous quantities of data can be handled quickly and easily, and they can be readily updated as new data become available.

### Seasonality

If we study cash commodity prices over an extended period of time on a month-to-month basis, we find that during certain months of the year price tends to top, whereas during other months price tends to bottom. Furthermore, during certain times of the year uptrends are common, while during other times of the year down-trends are common.

Each cash commodity market has its own seasonal price tendencies, but virtually all commodities follow a definite seasonal pattern. Because perishable commodities must be brought to market quickly, prices of those commodities tend to rise and fall as the product becomes more or less available. Anyone in the northern states who has had a taste for fresh strawberry shortcake in February knows that fresh strawberries are very expensive that time of the year, if any can be found at all. In May and June, however, fresh strawberry shortcake with whipped cream is a readily available and usually temptingly priced dessert.

Less perishable, storable commodities like the grains generally will be priced lowest at harvest time, as the available supply is relatively large in relationship to demand, but seasonal price moves of these commodities tend to be less volatile during the rest of the year than those of perishable commodities. Usually, with the grains, the price at times other than the harvest will reflect the price of the grains plus storage costs.

Monthly seasonal price tendencies can be charted for each commodity when the price history of that commodity is known. By comparing monthly average prices for a commodity over the history of that commodity, a chart can be developed like those in Figures 7-1 to 7-5. Each of these charts tells us the monthly seasonal price tendency for a particular commodity. If the plotted line in any of the charts is up in one of the months, we know that prices have a tendency to rise during that month. If the line moves down, prices have a downward tendency. The row of numbers along the bottom reveals the percentage of time that tendency has held true.

If we look at Figure 7-1, we find that wheat prices tend to fall from February until June and then rise through January. The most significant change occurs in October, however, where we find that 81% of the time

*Figure 7-1. Wheat Cash Monthly Seasonal Chart.*

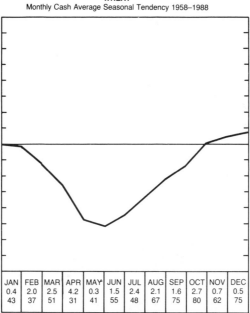

**WHEAT**
Monthly Cash Average Seasonal Tendency 1958–1988

| JAN | FEB | MAR | APR | MAY | JUN | JUL | AUG | SEP | OCT | NOV | DEC |
|-----|-----|-----|-----|-----|-----|-----|-----|-----|-----|-----|-----|
| 0.4 | 2.0 | 2.5 | 4.2 | 0.3 | 1.5 | 2.4 | 2.1 | 1.6 | 2.7 | 0.7 | 0.5 |
| 43  | 37  | 51  | 31  | 41  | 55  | 48  | 67  | 75  | 80  | 62  | 75  |

since 1936 wheat prices have gone up between October 1 and November 1.

## SEASONAL TENDENCIES IN FUTURES PRICES

A market analyst wishing to use the concept of *seasonality* for trading in the futures market, particularly a speculator who trades on a short-term basis, will find that charting seasonal tendencies of futures prices on a week-to-week or day-to-day basis is more suited to the needs of the short-term trader than is the monthly cash seasonal. In this case, seasonal futures tendencies are specific to the futures contract month. When we analyze the statistics for each futures month, we arrive at a chart that looks like Figure 7-6. Again, the direction of the plotted line reveals the seasonal tendency, up or down, but this time the figures along the bottom indicate the percentage of times prices closed up for the week.

Figure 7–2.   *Hogs Cash Monthly Seasonal Chart.*

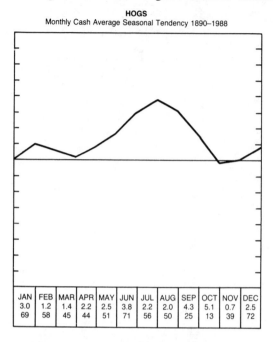

**HOGS**
Monthly Cash Average Seasonal Tendency 1890–1988

| JAN | FEB | MAR | APR | MAY | JUN | JUL | AUG | SEP | OCT | NOV | DEC |
|-----|-----|-----|-----|-----|-----|-----|-----|-----|-----|-----|-----|
| 3.0 | 1.2 | 1.4 | 2.2 | 2.5 | 3.8 | 2.2 | 2.0 | 4.3 | 5.1 | 0.7 | 2.5 |
| 69 | 58 | 45 | 44 | 51 | 71 | 56 | 50 | 25 | 13 | 39 | 72 |

Figure 7–3.   *Coffee Cash Monthly Seasonal Chart.*

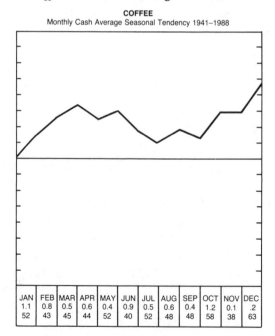

**COFFEE**
Monthly Cash Average Seasonal Tendency 1941–1988

| JAN | FEB | MAR | APR | MAY | JUN | JUL | AUG | SEP | OCT | NOV | DEC |
|-----|-----|-----|-----|-----|-----|-----|-----|-----|-----|-----|-----|
| 1.1 | 0.8 | 0.5 | 0.6 | 0.4 | 0.9 | 0.5 | 0.6 | 0.4 | 1.2 | 0.1 | .2 |
| 52 | 43 | 45 | 44 | 52 | 40 | 52 | 48 | 48 | 58 | 38 | 63 |

134

## Figure 7-4. Copper Cash Monthly Seasonal Chart.

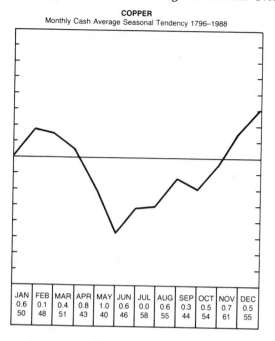

**COPPER**
Monthly Cash Average Seasonal Tendency 1796–1988

| JAN | FEB | MAR | APR | MAY | JUN | JUL | AUG | SEP | OCT | NOV | DEC |
|-----|-----|-----|-----|-----|-----|-----|-----|-----|-----|-----|-----|
| 0.6 | 0.1 | 0.4 | 0.8 | 1.0 | 0.6 | 0.0 | 0.6 | 0.3 | 0.5 | 0.7 | 0.5 |
| 50 | 48 | 51 | 43 | 40 | 46 | 58 | 55 | 44 | 54 | 61 | 55 |

## Figure 7-5. Canadian Dollar Cash Monthly Seasonal Chart.

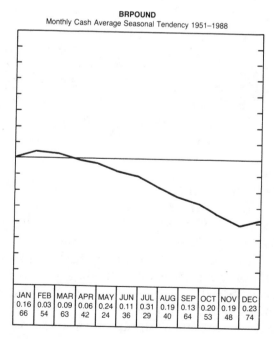

**BRPOUND**
Monthly Cash Average Seasonal Tendency 1951–1988

| JAN | FEB | MAR | APR | MAY | JUN | JUL | AUG | SEP | OCT | NOV | DEC |
|-----|-----|-----|-----|-----|-----|-----|-----|-----|-----|-----|-----|
| 0.16 | 0.03 | 0.09 | 0.06 | 0.24 | 0.11 | 0.31 | 0.19 | 0.13 | 0.20 | 0.19 | 0.23 |
| 66 | 54 | 63 | 42 | 24 | 36 | 29 | 40 | 64 | 53 | 48 | 74 |

135

Thus, a high number would indicate a high probability of prices closing up for a given week, whereas a low number would represent a high probability of prices closing down. By noting very high or very low numbers on the chart as I have done in Figure 7-7, the analyst can identify weeks that have had a very consistent seasonal tendency.

Because of the research that has gone into the development of these seasonal charts, I have been asked whether this kind of seasonal study is fundamental analysis or technical analysis. My reply is that seasonality is the most basic kind of fundamental, but I have studied it and used it in a very technical way. That is, I don't pay attention to what causes seasonal movement. I simply record the historical patterns of seasonality and use simple probability to predict future patterns.

## CYCLIC PRICE CHANGES

Prices of all commodities tend to repeat up-and-down trends in a relatively predictable fashion over a prescribed period of time. The cyclic method of analysis and forecasting has its roots in the work of Edward R. Dewey, founder of The Foundation for the Study of Cycles. With the advent of computer technology and its ease of access to the speculator, the use of price cycles has been popularized in recent years. And yet, cyclic analysis does not have many followers today.

For one thing, the application of cycles to the marketplace is not nearly as simple a matter as is the demonstration of their existence. Although the process of identifying price cycles from price data is fairly easy, the intricacies of cyclic analysis are such that a commitment must be made in order for a trader to achieve lasting success trading with this system. Even when a trader decides to use *cyclic analysis* as a method for trading in the markets, other timing devices and filters are nec-

Figure 7-6. *Sugar Weekly Seasonal Composite Futures Chart.*

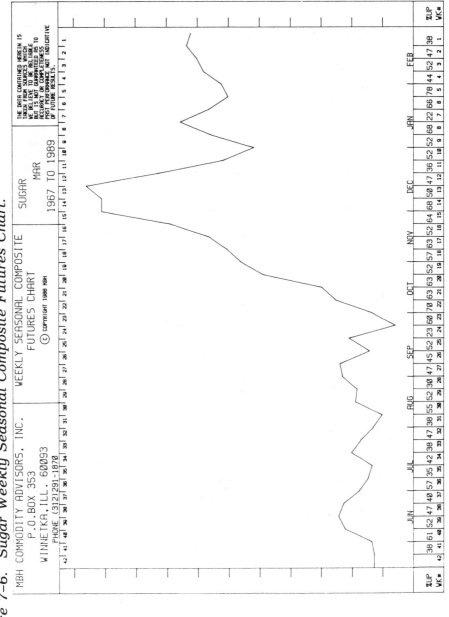

*Figure 7-7.  Corn Weekly Seasonal Composite Futures Chart.*

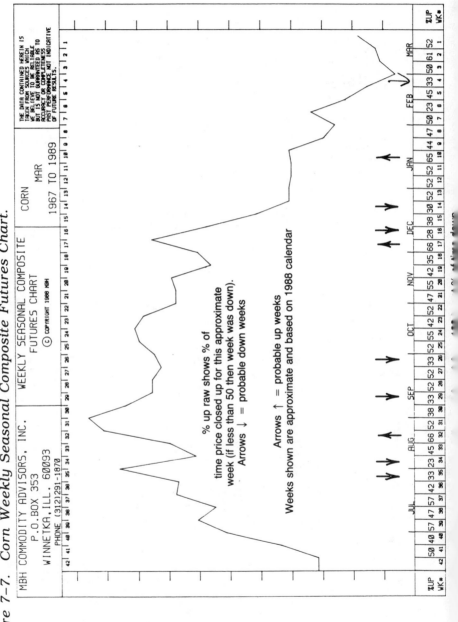

essary in order to get in and out of the market at the right times.

Much has been written about business cycles, price cycles, and the like. Suffice it to say that a proper understanding of price fundamentals requires a thorough knowledge of price cycles. It would be essential to know, for instance, that corn has a price cycle of approximately 5.7 years and that the low of that cycle occurred in early 1988, before making any predictions about corn prices based on estimates of supply and demand. There is also a 30- to 34-month price cycle in corn that must be considered.

Futures and cash prices demonstrate many different cyclic lengths, ranging from the ultralong term to the ultrashort term. On the short-term end of the spectrum, we have the approximately four- to five-day cycle in silver prices. On the long-term end of the continuum, we find the approximate 54-year cycle in most commodity prices; This number is about the longest cycle commodity traders study.

Figures 7-8 to 7-10 illustrate examples of various price cycles. Cycles are measured low to low, high to high, or low to high, and various types of measurements are possible. A more thorough understanding of price cycles, timing indicators, and cyclic theories may be obtained from my book, *The Handbook of Commodity Cycles: A Window on Time.*

Price cycles can vary considerably in length, thereby making it difficult if not impossible to make precise predictions about future behavior of the cycle. At times, there will even be an inversion of cyclic highs and lows with tops being made when lows should be made. This tends to occur when the market is at a major turning point.

Using cyclic analysis as a trading method requires: (1) projecting the cycles, (2) forecasting the next high or low, and (3) timing your entry into the market. Computer programs can help find cycles by matching dates and cycle lengths and testing them in the past, as well as

*Figure 7-8. Soybean Meal Monthly Futures.*

SOYBEAN MEAL
MONTHLY FUTURES

Chart reprinted with permission of
Commodity Price Charts
219 Parkade, Cedar Falls, IA. 50613

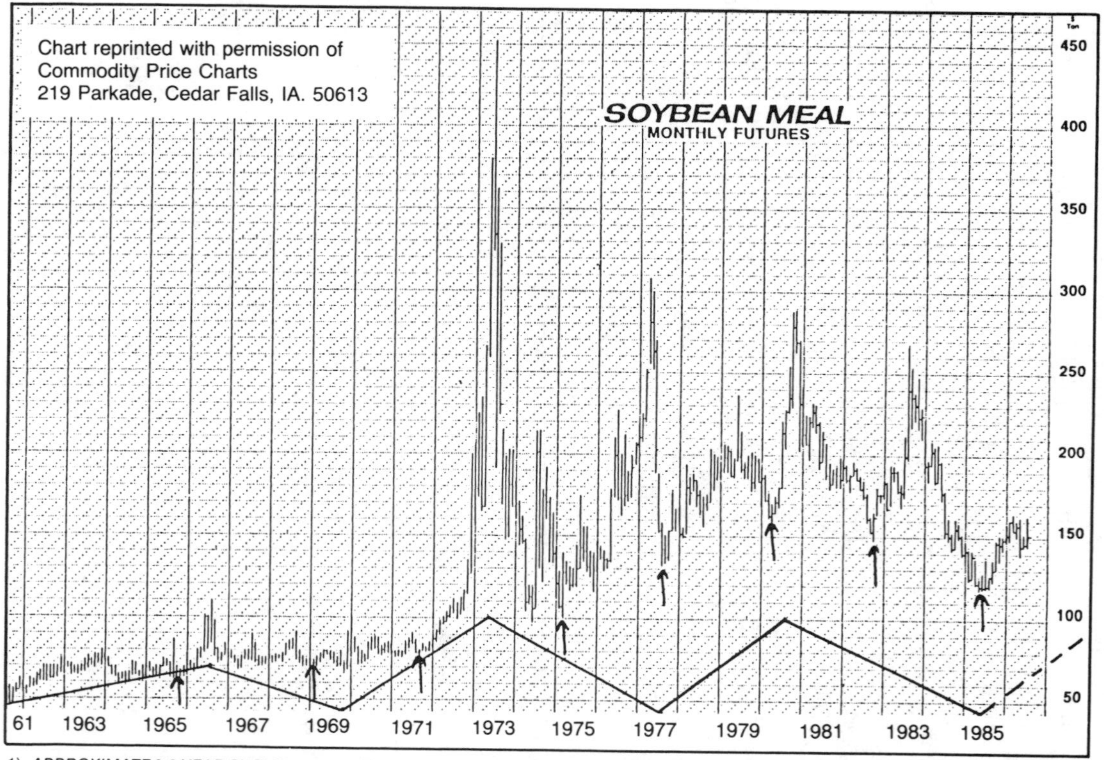

1) *APPROXIMATE 9.3 YEAR CYCLE lows* and highs are shown in chart at right and on the monthly cash average chart on page 11. The cycle has been a bit shorter in futures than in cash. Projections are given below.

tures chart at right. This is one of the most regular and reliable cycles in any of the markets. See projections below.

3) *EARLY DECADE LOWS* are also shown by arrows. This is a highly

2) *APPROXIMATE 20-26 MONTH CYCLE* ...

*Figure 7–9. Live Cattle Monthly Futures.*

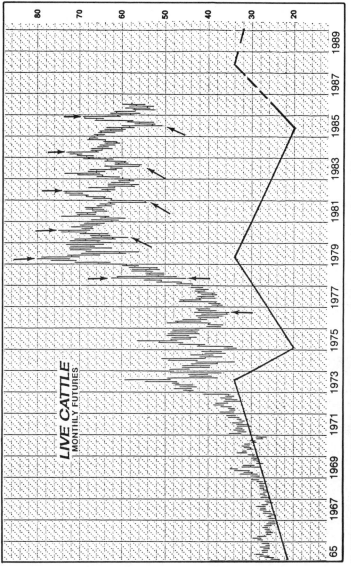

**LIVE CATTLE**
MONTHLY FUTURES

1) *APPROXIMATE MID-DECADE CYCLE:* The circled numbers 1-8 shows an approximate mid year decade low pattern in cattle prices (page 17). You will note how prices have bottomed near mid decade during the 4th through 6th year after the start of each decade. Though this pattern is not perfect it is also one observed in hog prices. The tendency after a mid decade low has been for prices to increase by a significant amount thereafter, usually topping about 2 years prior to the end of the decade in the years number 7, 8, 9.

2) *APPROXIMATE 10.6 YEAR CYCLE* is also shown at the bottom of chart on page 17. This cycle has likely bottomed in 1985 with the mid decade cycle described above.

3) *APPROXIMATE 19-22 MONTH CYCLES* are shown below with arrows marking recent highs and lows. The last two approximate 10.6 year cycle are shown on the MONTHLY FUTURES CHART below and projected through the next probable top (based on the top tendency mentioned in #1 above).

141

*Figure 7-10. Copper Monthly Futures.*

1) *APPROXIMATE 12.8 YEAR CYCLE* lows and highs are shown on page 31. This cycle has been somewhat variable at times, but it is fairly reliable overall. It suggests that a low was made in 1984, yet a low even at this time would still be within reasonable bounds of the cycle length. A top is due in the early 1990's.

2) *EARLY DECADE LOW PATTERN.* Copper has shown a tendency to make lows early in each decade, most often in the years numbered 2 or 3. Though the subsequent upmove may at times be small, it does, nevertheless, appear to be consistent (lows marked 1-7).

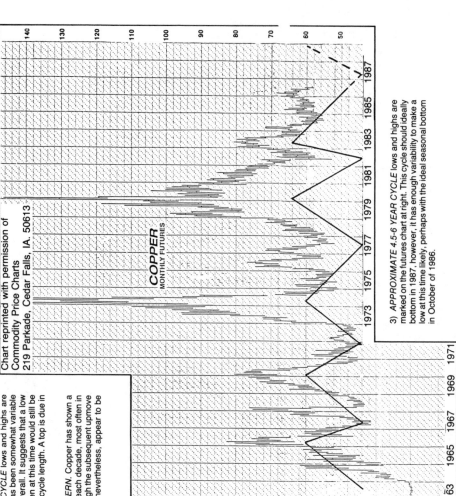

Chart reprinted with permission of
Commodity Price Charts
219 Parkade, Cedar Falls, IA. 50613

COPPER
MONTHLY FUTURES

3) *APPROXIMATE 4.5-6 YEAR CYCLE* lows and highs are marked on the futures chart at right. This cycle should ideally bottom in 1987, however, it has enough variability to make a low at this time likely, perhaps with the ideal seasonal bottom in October of 1986.

142

projecting them into the future. Once the cycle has been identified, simply counting into the future establishes a time frame or time window during which the cycle should ideally top or bottom. A suitable timing indicator then gives the signal to enter the market. Figures 7-11 to 7-13 illustrate a few of the timing indicators that can be effective when the cyclic top or bottom is imminent.

Although cyclic analysis is fascinating, using it as a specific trading system is not recommended for the novice trader.

*Figure 7–11.  Timing Signals, Upside and Downside Reversals.*

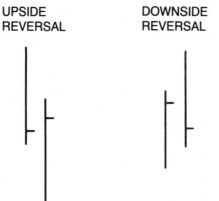

UPSIDE
REVERSAL

DOWNSIDE
REVERSAL

*Figure 7–12.   Timing Signals.*

LOW-HIGH CLOSE

HIGH-LOW CLOSE

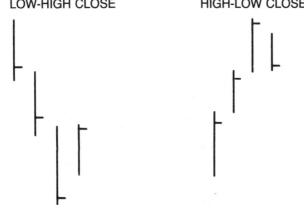

*Figure 7-13.   Timing Signals on Closing Basis Charts.*

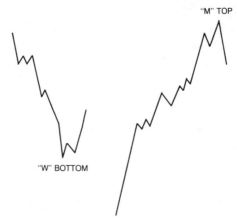

## SECULAR TRENDS

Less predictable than seasonals and cycles but significant nevertheless as an influence on prices are price trends resulting from long-term changes in supply and demand. Such changes as demographic movements, long-term weather changes, changes in customs and tastes, government policies, the discovery of new uses for a commodity, and large-scale changes in consumer purchasing power may move prices of a commodity into a different range than it previously traded in.

Other secular trends can be created by crop substitution, reevaluation of the dollar, new technology, and increasing or decreasing the available crop acreage. Such secular trends must be taken into account in any long-range prediction of price movement.

### Government Price Support

The government is an ever-present but often fickle influence on commodity prices. Because of its tendency to react much too slowly and to respond all too often to political issues, the government can often exacerbate rather than solve market problems. Nevertheless, government programs have a significant influence—in some cases the most significant influence—on the prices of commodities. Through loans to farmers, acreage allotments, direct cash incentive plans, programs to dispose of surplus crops and programs to take land out of production altogether, the government intervenes in myriad ways with the market economy.

### Government Reports

I mentioned earlier the market and price reports published periodically by the USDA. The government also publishes many other reports about the economy that may have a strong effect on commodity prices. For example, the monthly balance of trade report in October 1987 seemed to be a catalyst for the stock market crash that month. The various reports on wholesale prices, consumer prices, trade deficits, unemployment, money supply, stockpiles of goods (the list goes on), all have a more or less direct and more or less significant effect on prices.

### Political Decisions

Political decisions anywhere in the world may affect commodity prices significantly. In many developing countries, the government may elect to support the price of a particular commodity in order to enhance its value on the world market. Other countries may adopt protectionist attitudes, which result in tariffs and other trade barriers, to protect local producers from outside competition. President Carter's decision to embargo grain shipments to the Soviet Union in 1979, as a result of the Soviet invasion of Afghanistan, had an immediate depressive impact on the farm economy in the United States by depriving farmers of huge markets for their grain.

### Weather

Weather patterns will cause prices to vary during a growing season. A dry spring establishes expectations for a crop shortfall. A late freeze creates the probability of reduced production. A freeze in South America during the time that is winter in the northern hemisphere can cause future prices to shoot up, particularly in soybeans, coffee, and orange juice.

Weather affects commodity prices primarily during the growing season. However, because of what amounts to a worldwide market, it seems that the growing season now stretches year-round, and weather anywhere on the planet can have an effect on the price of one commodity or another.

### International News

Many of the imported commodities, such as sugar, copper, platinum, wool, coffee, and cocoa, are particularly vulnerable to news of war or international tensions. News of war can lead to hoarding, as well as a greater demand for raw materials for defense and stockpiling. Moreover, there is the possibility of imports being cut off. On the other hand, the prospect of losing major export markets can significantly depress the prices of domestically produced commodities.

### Fluctuation of the Dollar

In the turbulent arena of foreign trade, the critical factor in the profitability of sales is more than ever the exchange rate of currencies. When the dollar is strong against foreign currencies, exports from the United States are more expensive and therefore less desirable. As the dollar declines, American goods become more competitive on the world market, and exports tend to increase. As foreign markets open up, however, demand for some commodity might increase, leading to a rise in prices domestically. It is possible to envision the unlikely scenario of commodity prices rising domestically while actually becoming more competitive internationally.

## General Business Conditions

When the economy is healthy, unemployment is low, the experts are predicting prosperous times ahead, and business is expanding, demand tends to be high for commodities. People are more willing to spend their money during optimistic times.

But when the specter of recession arises, unemployment creeps up, business slows, and people become nervous about the future, demand falls. Consumers become less willing to spend as freely.

## PRICE ANALYSIS

The individual who is serious about analyzing price by the fundamentals has quite a job. He must first determine the general business climate, whether it is inflationary or recessionary, whether unemployment is rising or falling. Next, he must check the trend of commodity prices by looking at one or more of the following: the Consumer Price Index, the Farm Price Index, the Dow Jones Averages, the Futures Price Indexes, the Reuters Spot Index, or the Commodity Research Bureau Futures Price Index.

After checking the general situation, the specific circumstances regarding individual commodities must be checked: When is the seasonal price pattern? What is the long-term price trend? What about government price supports? Expert subsidies? What are the figures on current production and carryover stocks? What are the prospects for demand domestically? What about foreign production? Currency exchange rates? Foreign political situations? Are there weather circumstances that are significant?

Fortunately for many fundamental analysts, there are computer programs that factor in much of the above information and develop price forecasts. Even with computer help, however, anyone who has the desire to be a fundamental analyst must feel overwhelmed at times by the scope of the information that must be processed and the number of variables that must be considered.

The large brokerage houses and the large producers and users generally have the resources to maintain the staff and the equipment to carry out adequate analysis of all of the fundamental forces that move the market. The average futures trader will find it more difficult, if not impossible, to carry on effective fundamental analysis. Even the most sophisticated of systems will not be perfect. There will always be unexpected variables acting on the market that the system missed. I have always maintained that the market works perfectly as it responds to all of the various forces that act upon it. It is we who try to interpret those forces who are often imperfect.

CHAPTER 8

# The Basics of Technical Analysis

The futures market is essentially a laboratory for the study of group psychology. When we discussed fundamental analysis of the futures market, we made the point that price is determined by the interplay of supply and demand. This concept seems straightforward enough until we encounter such complications as elasticity of demand and elasticity of supply. What creates elasticity in supply and demand? Human nature does.

Consumers are quite varied in their perceptions of what constitutes a good price, or when an item is a bargain, or, for that matter, when they can afford a particular item. Two individuals making an identical salary will be totally at odds when it comes to a decision regarding whether or not they can afford a new car, for instance. Obviously, when purchasing decisions are being made, much more enters into the decision than simple supply and demand. As an example, an individual who just received a 15% increase in salary might be inclined to shop for a new car, but if this same person encounters a rumor that the company is having problems and might be laying off 20% of the work force, the decision to buy the new car will likely be deferred.

Similarly, in the futures market, any two individuals can perceive the same fundamental information and arrive at opposite conclusions regarding the impact of that information on prices. In fact, it is that phenomenon that creates a futures marketplace. Since the activity of speculating in futures contracts requires a buyer and a seller, there must always exist opposing forecasts of price moves for there to be a liquid market or one in which transactions can occur quickly and easily.

Many traders in the futures market believe that the patterns of group behavior in the futures market can be recorded and studied and that predictions regarding futures behavior can be made based on recurring patterns. In other words, it might be possible to overlook fundamental information and focus entirely on the patterns of price movement because these patterns reflect the behavior of the participants, and people's behavior tends to repeat itself.

*CHARTS*

People who chart prices in the futures market generally use one of two kinds of charts: the *bar chart* or the *point-and-figure chart*. Each has its advantages and liabilities.

## The Bar Chart

If you have ever seen a price chart of the futures market or, for that matter, the stock market, you probably have seen a bar chart. This particular chart is designed to provide three specific characteristics of price during a particular trading period: the opening price, the closing price, and the range of prices from high to low through which trading occurred during the trading period. A price bar might represent a period as short as five minutes or as long as a month. The most common is the daily bar chart.

Figure 8-1 presents a typical price bar. The vertical bar represents the range of trading for that particular day. The highest price of the day is at point A, and the lowest price of the day is at point B. The horizontal line intersecting the price bar from the left is the opening price. On this day, the opening price is shown by C. Conversely, the horizontal line intersecting the price bar from the right is the closing price. On this day, the closing price is shown at point D.

## The Point-and-Figure Chart

A point-and-figure chart resembles a game of tic-tac-toe, with all its boxes filled with either an x or an o. Actually, it is a chart whose purpose is to provide information not included in a bar chart. Whereas the bar hart records price range during a specified time period, a point-and-figure chart doesn't record time; rather, this kind of chart records reversals in prices of a commodity.

As price moves up, it is recorded as an x in the price boxes. As price moves down, it is recorded in the price box as an o. As the person who builds the point-and-figure chart, you can decide the value of each box in the chart. If you want a very sensitive chart that records most of the price action, each box can be worth one tic on the price of the commodity. A less sensitive chart can be developed using other increments, e.g., one cent versus one-quarter cent.

As the chart builder, you can also decide when prices will be recorded: every time they occur or only when certain larger moves have occurred. For example, a point-and-figure chart in corn might register a price change of one cent per bushel, with each box being worth one-quarter cent. Then an x would be entered only when price advanced one cent, but four boxes would be filled in when a one-cent move occurred (Figure 8-2).

However, the primary function of the point-and-figure chart is to record price reversals. The procedure is to continue marking an x (if the price is rising) or an o (if the price is falling) until a significant price reversal occurs. Again, you decide what is a significant price reversal. Obviously, you would not consider a one-tic reversal significant. If it were, the chart would be filled with meaningless x's and o's.

*Figure 8-1.  Price Bar, July Hogs.*

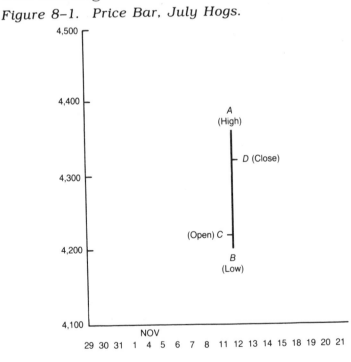

To avoid too many reversals, you might decide that three tics, or three boxes on the chart, is a significant reversal. When the price moved at least three tics in the opposite direction from the last entry, that reversal would be registered by filling in o's next to the appropriate prices if the reversal was down or x's if the reversal was up. For normal use, a three-box reversal chart, as described, is probably unrealistic to keep unless you are on the floor or right next to a quote machine. Unless there is a need for such close monitoring of a market, boxes of higher value should be used, so that fewer entries will be made.

*Figure 8–2. December Corn Point-and-Figure Chart, 4 × 1.*

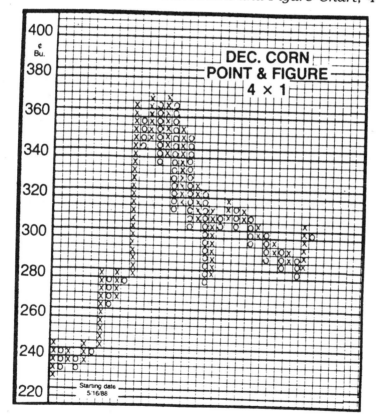

Courtesy of Commodity Price Charts, 219 Parkade Cedar Falls, IA 50613.

## CHART PATTERNS

Because price charts register human behavior as it is communicated through price changes of commodities, certain patterns of price movement recur often enough and are associated with certain outcomes with sufficient frequency to be considered significant predictors of price movement.

### Trends

The elementary information that every technical analyst wants to know first is the price *trend:* the long-term trend, the intermediate trend, the short-term trend. Perhaps the most frequent mistake made in the futures market is to follow a trade signal of one kind or another without considering the current trend. "Bucking the trend" can be deadly. Establishing an accurate trend line, however, is not necessarily an easy task. Different chart analysts will use different materials or choose different points on the chart by which to draw a trend line.

Figure 8-3 demonstrates a clear trend line, showing a definite bull trend in the hog futures market. Notice that for many weeks prices remained above their "support" trend line. When prices topped and turned lower, they remained below their "resistance" trend line for many weeks.

### Reversal Patterns

Several chart patterns are indicators of trend reversals (changes) and signal a price *top* or *bottom.* In a price top, the number of available buyers declines, and sellers begin to dominate the market, causing prices, which had been rising, to begin falling. In a price bottom, conversely, buyers begin to dominate the market, reversing the recent downtrend in prices.

One of the most reliable reversal patterns is the "head-and-shoulders" formation, which looks much like

*Figure 8–3. Trend Line in Hog Futures.*

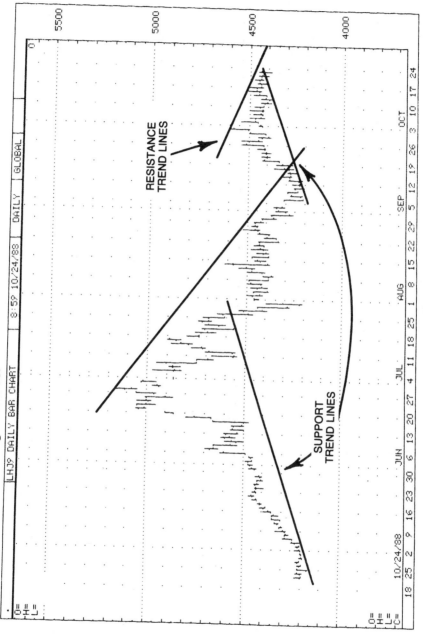

a "w," with an extended center leg (Figure 8-4). In a typical head-and-shoulders top, prices rally and decline at *A*, forming the left shoulder. They then rally again at *B* as buyers try once again to maintain the bull market trend. This second rally sends prices higher than the shoulder, forming the head. As prices fall back again, the third rally at *C* is not able to reach the price level at *B*, forming the right shoulder. At this point, sellers have assumed the stronger position in the market, and as prices penetrate the "neckline" (1), a bear market ensues.

Another reversal pattern is the triangle formation (Figure 8-5). An ascending triangle, as shown, following an extended decline, is a signal that prices have bottomed. Although rising prices encounter resistance at *A*, buying pressure increases on each rally until a breakout finally occurs at *B*. Similarly, a descending triangle following an extended uptrend will often signal a market top.

Price gaps, as shown in Figure 8-6, can be useful in chart analysis. A common assumption is that gaps will be filled; that is, sooner or later prices will trade in the range left open by the price gap. Chartists will designate common gaps, breakaway gaps, measuring gaps, runaway gaps, and exhaustion gaps.

Other chart formations include key reversals (Figure 8-7), island reversals (Figure 8-8), double tops and bottoms (Figure 8-9), flags and pennants (Figure 8-10), saucer bottoms, and triangles. To the trained eye, these formations can provide significant information. Often, however, as the patterns are forming, one can only speculate as to what is actually occurring. The formations are much easier to define after they are completed, which, of course, is often too late to be of significant value. Thus, the reading of chart formations is often more an art than a science.

However, it is possible—and more traders and commodity trading advisors are doing this—to feed massive amounts of historical price data into a computer and

*Figure 8-4. Head-and-Shoulders Top Formation.*

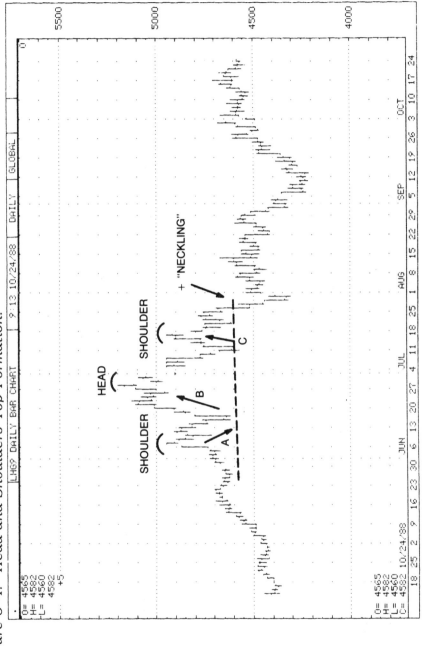

Figure 8-5. Ascending Triangle Following Extended Decline.

*Figure 8-6.  Price Gaps.*

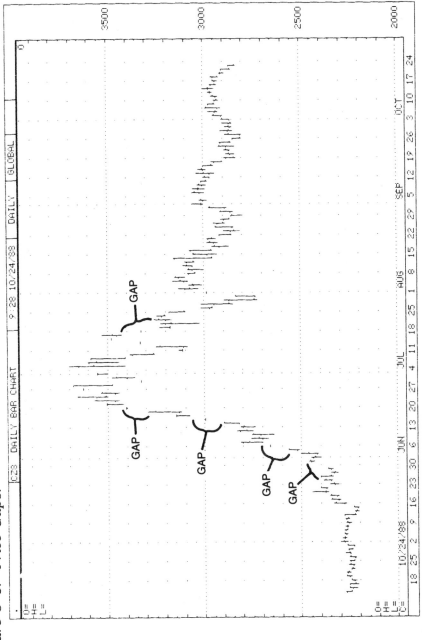

*Figure 8-7.  Key Reversal.*

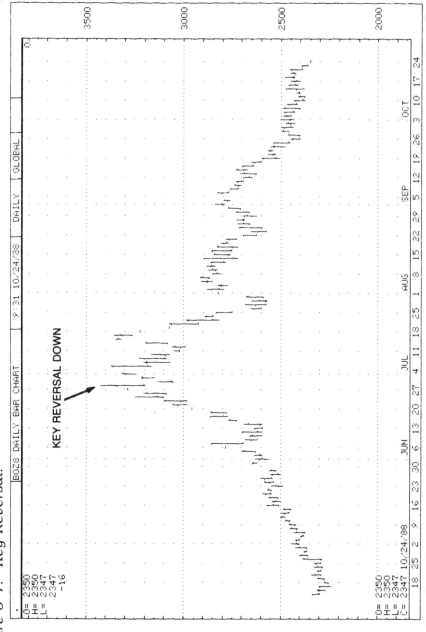

*Figure 8-8.  Island Reversal.*

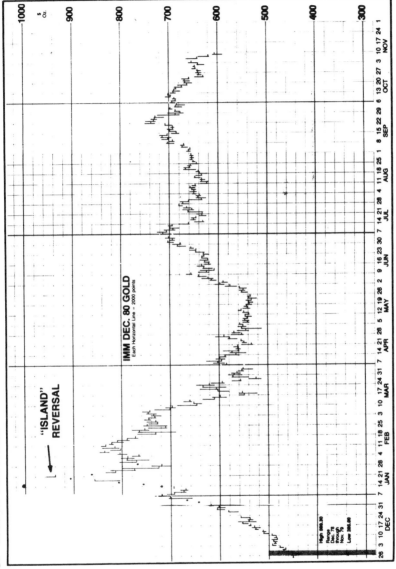

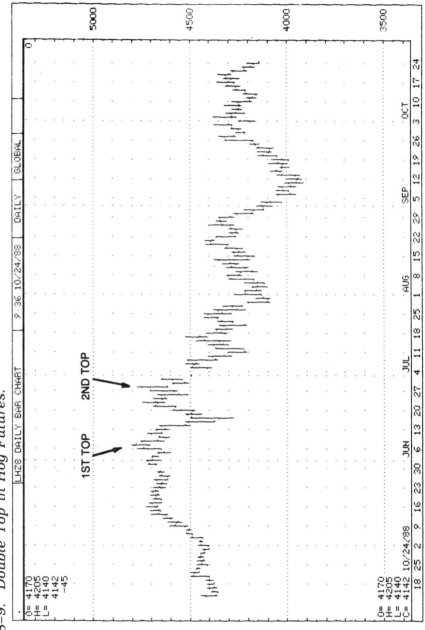

Figure 8-9.  Double Top in Hog Futures.

*Figure 8–10. Flag/Pennant.*

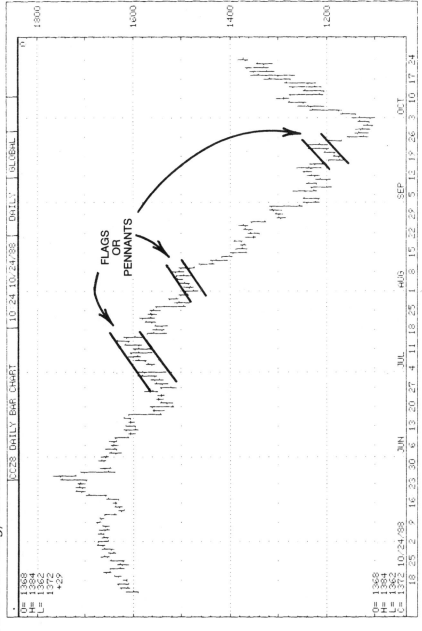

thus improve the probabilities of concretely recognizing certain patterns. Accurate pattern recognition can lead to higher accuracy of trading.

## TIMING OF TRADES

Good chart reading can provide a great deal of valuable information about the price trend and significant price trend reversals. This information alone, however, is not sufficient to make good trades. A successful trader must know how to time the trades in order to get into the market at the right time to catch the move he is looking for. A number of techniques are available to assist in the timing of trades.

Among the more well-known and more frequently used techniques are moving averages, relative strength indicator (RSI), oscillators, and stochastics. Each of these is a system for using past price information to generate buying and selling signals.

## MOVING AVERAGES

Trend lines and chart patterns provide obvious assistance to the technical analyst. Both are useful for predicting futures market moves. Unfortunately, both chart patterns and trend lines are subjective in nature. Two analysts can view the same chart and find two different patterns and two different trend lines. What is needed is a more objective system for defining trend and for providing more precise entry and exit signals.

In the 1950s, Richard Donchain advanced the notion that a different type of trend line could be used to establish buy-and-sell signals, as well as indications of support and resistance. Rather than the familiar (straight-line) trend method, Donchain advanced the notion that a *moving average* of price could be constructed in order to provide market timing indicators.

A moving average is a simple mathematical manipulation of raw data that provides up-to-date or moving indications of market activity. Instead of examining price highs and lows for the entire history of the current contract, a moving average constantly progresses and examines only a defined segment of time, particularly in the recent past.

A 10-day moving average, for example, will only look at prices for the last 10 days, ignoring what has transpired before. In so doing, it provides a more sensitive measure by taking an average of the worth of prices over the last 10 days and on the 11th day dropping the oldest day in the data and recalculating the average with the current daily data. At any given point and time, only 10 days of data are used. However, they are the most recent 10 days.

The calculations for a moving average are very simple and straightforward. For a 10-day moving average, simply add the 10 most recent closing prices and divide that sum by 10. The following day, drop the last price in the series and add the current price. Again, divide the sum by 10. On each succeeding day, repeat the calculation. Before long, if each day's moving average is plotted and connected, you will have a fluctuating trend line that follows the price line (Figure 8-11).

A moving average of prices may be calculated using any number of periods (e.g., two-day, three-day, 10-day, 14-day period) or any period length (e.g., five-minute, 10-minute, hourly, daily, weekly, monthly length). Theoreticaly, if the daily price is consistently higher than the moving average of prices, it means prices are trending upward (bullish). Conversely, if the daily price is consistently lower than the moving average, the trend is lower (bearish). When the daily price line crosses the moving average line, however, it might mean a change in the price trend (Figure 8-12), which might be a signal to take action in the market.

As you can see in Figure 8-13, the moving average makes its direction changes after the daily price has

Figure 8–11. Moving Average Line and Price Bars.

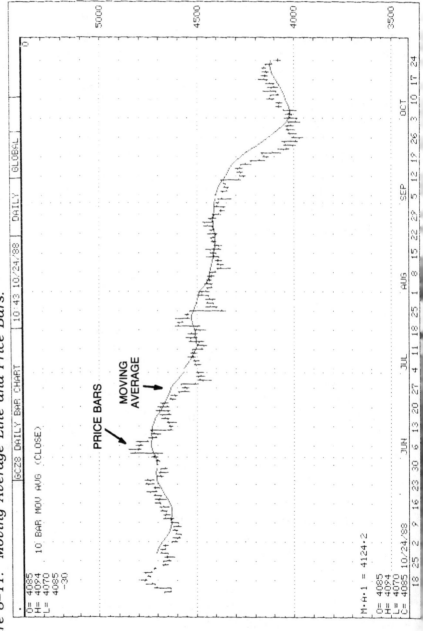

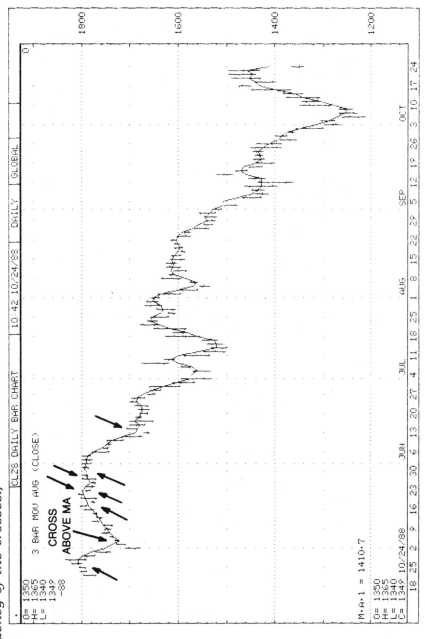

*Figure 8–12. Three-Day Moving Average with Price Line Crossing Moving Average Signaling Trend Change. (Note that not all crosses are shown and, in particular, note the high frequency of the crosses.)*

already changed direction. The greater the number of periods included in the moving average, the more it lags behind the daily price movement (compare Figure 8-14, a three-day moving average, with Figure 8-15, a 14-day moving average).

Notice that as the number of periods in the moving average increases, the fluctuations in price action become smoother: The moving average tends to reduce the effect of price variations. Notice also that daily prices may go one way while the moving average is going the other: Prices may go lower while the moving average continues higher, and vice versa.

### Using the Moving Average

A technical analyst will use the moving average in various ways. The moving average alone is used like a flexible trend line: While the moving average is increasing, the trader maintains a long position, and vice versa. When the moving average reverses direction, the trader liquidates the position. Though useful, this technique will unfortunately miss most of a market move because of the delay before the moving average changes direction.

To reduce the delay, a moving average can be used in conjunction with the daily price. As Figures 8-16 to 8-18 clearly show, the daily price line will often cross the moving average line, and the number of crossings increase as the number of periods in the moving average decrease. These crossings can provide market signals. When the moving average changes direction, a new position may be taken. When the price line crosses the moving average, the position is liquidated. Used this way, the signal occurs much earlier, and a position may be taken that will catch more of a market move.

An even more sensitive use of the moving average is to combine it with a bar chart. Used this way, a moving average of the highs and a moving average of the lows will create a channel called a *volatility band* (Figure 8-19). When prices move out of this channel (point *A*, point

*Figure 8-13. Moving Average Making Direction Change.*

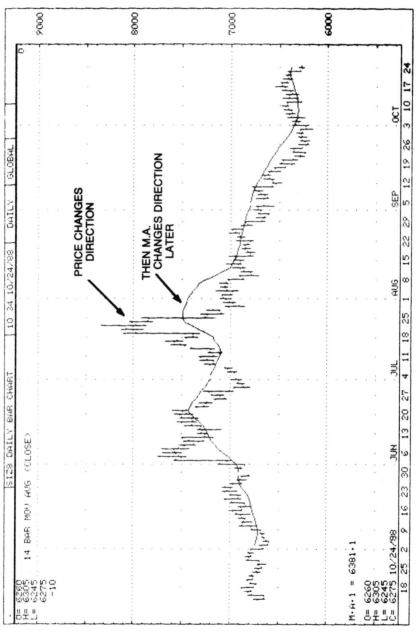

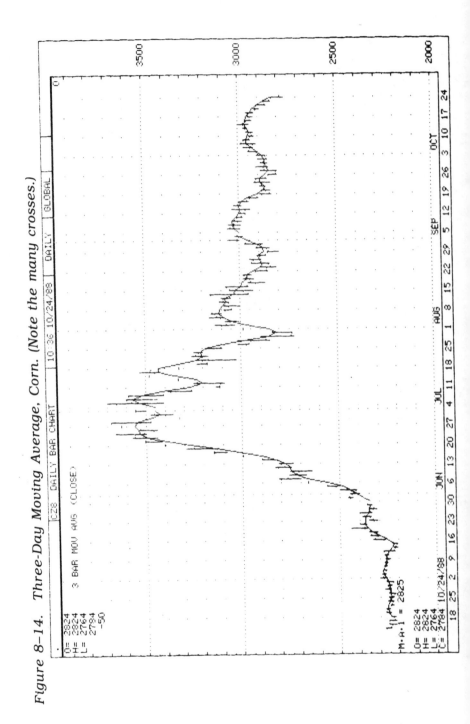

*Figure 8–14. Three-Day Moving Average, Corn. (Note the many crosses.)*

*Figure 8–15. Fourteen-Day Moving Average, Corn. (Note fewer signals than for three-period average.)*

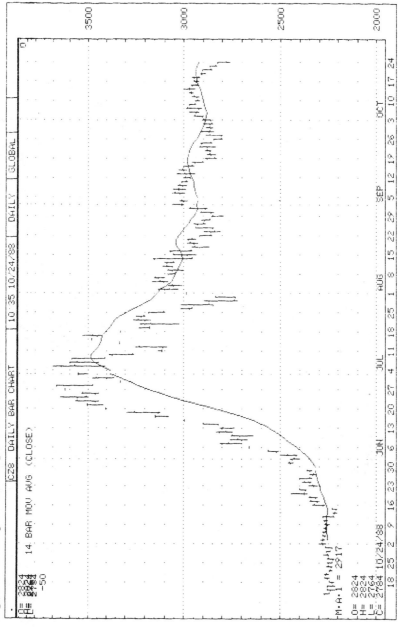

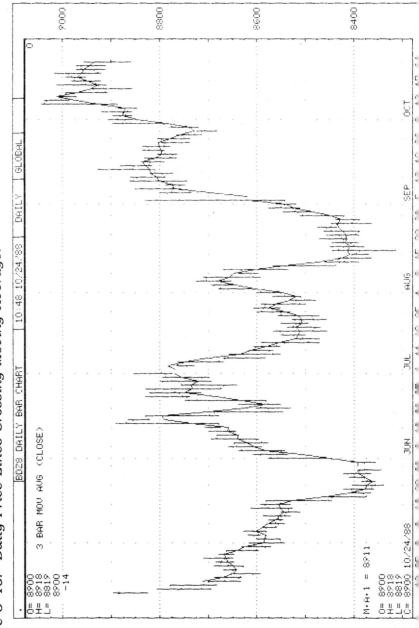

*Figure 8-16. Daily Price Lines Crossing Moving Average.*

*Figure 8-17. Daily Price Lines Crossing Moving Average.*

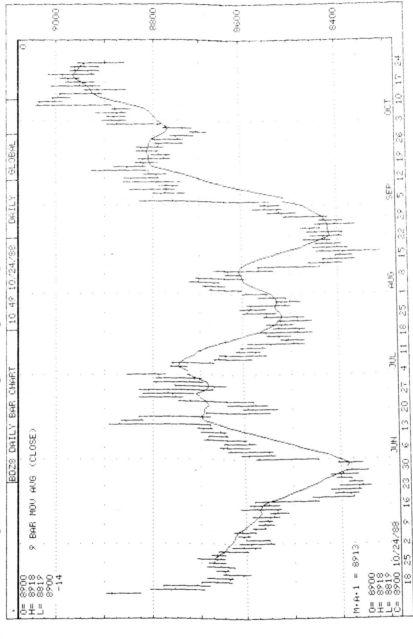

*Figure 8-18. Daily Price Lines Crossing Moving Average.*

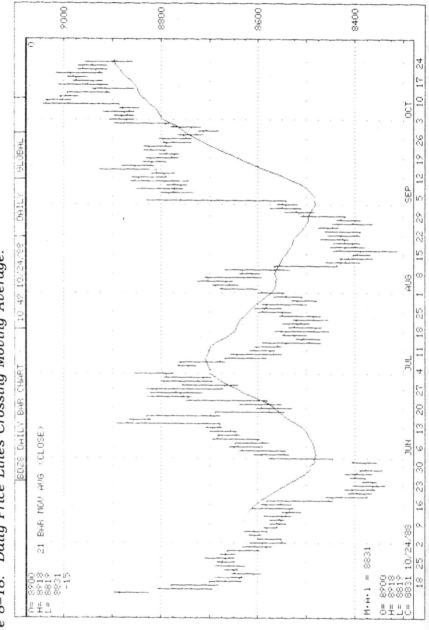

*B*), a new trend may be developing. When prices are outside the channel for two consecutive days, this may constitute a signal to take market action.

### Multiple Moving Averages

Many analysts have found that a single moving average is not accurate enough to use as a timing device, particularly in choppy markets (Figure 8-20). In such markets, a trader can get whipsawed back and forth by false signals and lose a great deal of money in the process. To help solve that problem, analysts will often use more than one moving average. When two moving averages are used together (Figure 8-21), the longer moving average—in this case, a 10-day average—can define the trend while the shorter moving average (a three-day average, in this example) provides timing signals.

A further refinement is to use three moving averages. Specifically, the four-day, nine-day, and 18-day averages seem to work best together. Figures 8-22 to 8-24 show this combination, and the signals that can be generated from its application. With this system, a signal is theoretically given when the nine-day average crosses the 18-day average. To avoid false signals, the four-day moving average should be higher than the nine-day average for a legitimate buy signal and below the nine-day average for a legitimate sell signal (Figure 8-25).

### Variations on the Moving Average

One variation I have found to have potential is to use a moving average of the opening prices rather than the closing ones. Other analysts will use a moving average of the average of the high-low closing prices. Sometimes, it is helpful, when using a volatility band of high and low prices, to use different periods for each moving average. For example, a 10-period average of the lows and a 14-period average of the highs provides quicker signals as prices move down. Such a combination may

*Figure 8–19. Volatility Band Channel of Moving Average
of Highs and Moving Average of Lows.*

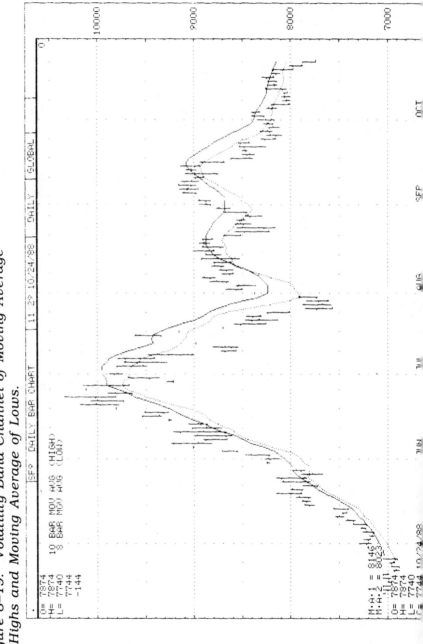

*Figure 8–20. Moving Average in Narrow Trading Range. (Note whipsaw signals.)*

O= 2490
H= 2490
L= 2432
   -75

18 BAR MOV AVG. (CLOSE)

M·A·1 = 2586·2

O= 2490
H= 2490
L= 2432
C= 2432  10/24/88

3500

3000

2500

2000

0

18  25   2   9  16  23  30   6  13  20  27   4  11  18  25   1   8  15  22  29   5  12  19  26   3  10  17  24
          JUN                  JUL                 AUG                 SEP                 OCT

177

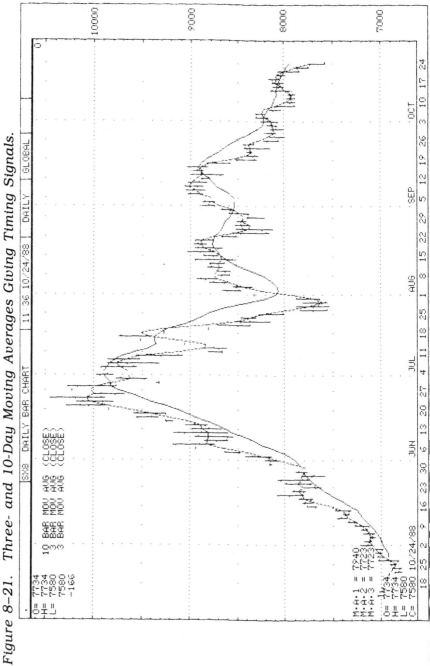

*Figure 8-21. Three- and 10-Day Moving Averages Giving Timing Signals.*

*Figure 8–22. Four-, Nine-, and 18-Day Moving Averages with Signals.*

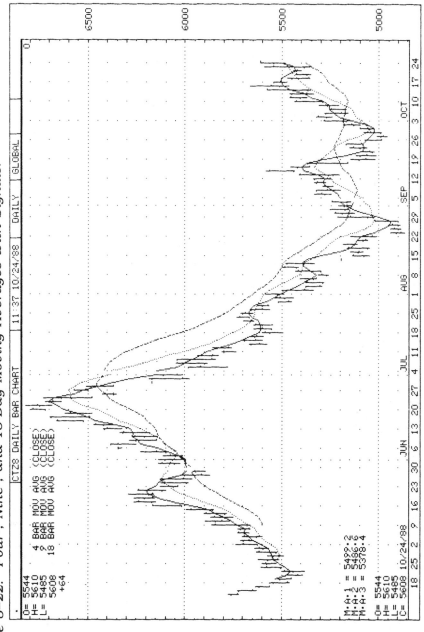

*Figure 8-23. Four-, Nine-, and 18-Day Moving Averages with Signals.*

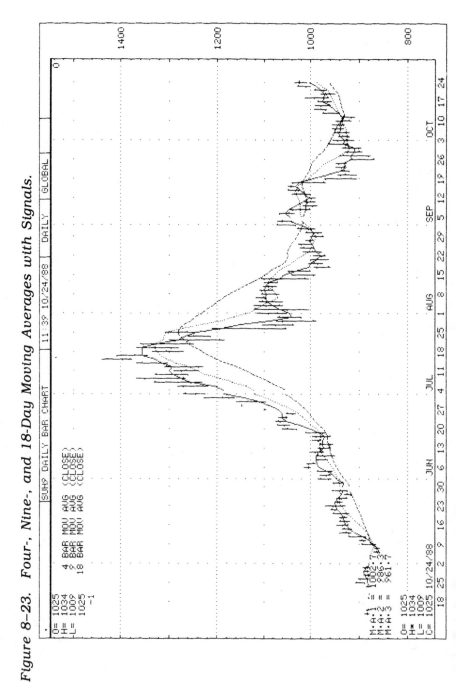

*Figure 8-24.  Four-, Nine-, and 18-Day Moving Averages with Signals.*

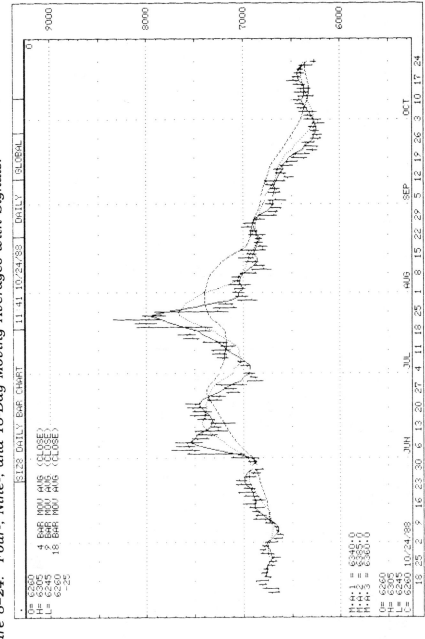

*Figure 8-25. Ten-Day Moving Average of Lows and 14-Day Moving Average of Highs.*

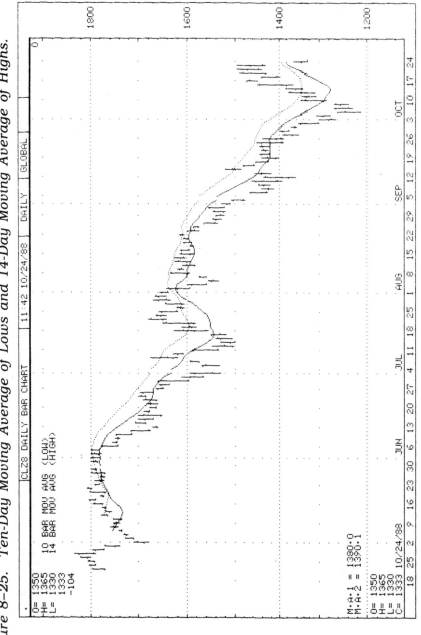

provide quicker entry signals, but slower exit signals, allowing the trader to take more profits from a position.

As sophisticated computers have become more readily available over the past few years, even more exotic combinations of moving averages have become practical to use. One such variation is the weighted moving average, which gives more importance to the nearby prices. As an example, in a 10-day moving average, the nearest price is multiplied by 10, the next by nine, and so on. The sum of all those values is divided by the sum of the multipliers, in this case, 55 (10 + 9 + 8 . . . + 1).

Another form of the weighted moving average is the geometric moving average. Without attempting to describe the complex mathematics involved in calculating this moving average, suffice it to say that it gives greater weight to the lower values in the series, and it is most useful in conjunction with long-term historic data that exhibit wide variance. This type of moving average will utilize quarterly or yearly prices.

The exponentially smoothed moving average uses all past data, rather than a limited number of periods, to calculate a value. Because a smoothing constant is used in the formula, price data is of diminishing significance the older it becomes. Thus, the exponential moving average is a variation of the weighted moving average.

A smoothing constant of 0.50 in the formula gives 50% of the total value of the price data to the current price, 25% to the next, 12.5% to the third, and so on. A constant of 0.50 is roughly equivalent to a three-day moving average. A 0.10 constant is equivalent to a 20-day moving average. The primary difference between a simple moving average and an exponentially smoothed moving average is that prices impact indefinitely on the exponential moving average.

Some analysts like to plot on the moving average so that it leads price rather than following it (Figure 8-26). Others like to center the moving average over the price. Altering the position in this way will change the timing of the signals.

*Figure 8–26.  Moving Average Leading Price.*

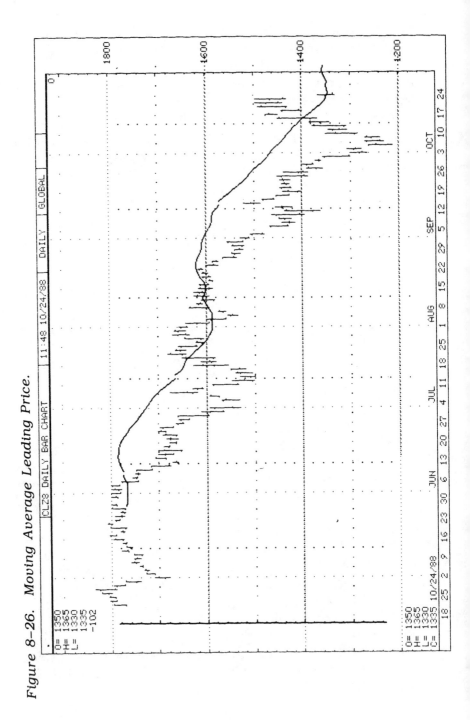

Many analysts have attempted to develop optimized moving averages for each market. Although more readily done these days with the proliferation of computer software and the increasing sophistication of market quote systems (it is possible now to hit a few keys on a keyboard and construct almost unlimited moving average combinations using real-time price data), such a process requires a great deal of time and must be monitored closely as market conditions change. What works today may not work tomorrow. What works in a trending market may not work in a sideways, or choppy, market.

With all the sophistication and variation attached to moving averages, studies have shown that a simple moving average seems to outperform linearly weighted and exponentially smoothed moving averages. Furthermore, the use of two moving averages seems to be the best combination, whereas a longer-range moving average is probably better than a shorter-range average, although a shorter moving average may be better suited to choppy markets.

### Conclusions About Moving Averages

Moving average signals are popular among many money managers and speculators. Their popularity derives from the fact that moving average signals meet many of the specific criteria of effective systems. These are as follows:

*1.* Moving average signals are specific and objective and almost force traders to follow the rules.

*2.* Moving average signals can keep the trader in the market at all times: closing out a long when going short and covering a short when going long. This is valuable, since the trader will thus be in a position when major moves begin.

*3.* Moving averages are trend-following systems. In other words, when a good trend is in effect, the likelihood of the moving average having a position consistent with the trend is very high.

Additionally, moving averages are quite easy to use in this age of computers. In fact, a computer can quite easily be programmed to generate specific buy-and-sell signals with various moving averages. The variations are endless. Moving averages are not predictors of market action, however. A moving average is a follower, not a leader. It never anticipates; it only reacts.

The best moving average for a hedger is probably not the same as for a speculator. A hedger probably would prefer a longer-range moving average, while a speculator would choose a shorter-range, more sensitive one. A portfolio manager, on the other hand, might prefer a longer-range moving average than a professional trader would.

Here are some important things to remember about moving averages:

*1.* A moving average is a follower, not a leader.

*2.* A moving average can never be precise; it will rarely generate signals that enter or exit a position at just the right price.

*3.* The speed of a moving average will change its profitability because it alters the size of profits and losses from each trade and it affects the accuracy and reliability of the system.

*4.* A moving average system is not designed to catch the beginning or end of the move. It will extract profits from the middle of a trend and will hold losses to a minimum, if used correctly.

*5.* In a sideways, or choppy, market, moving averages do not work well. In such a market, prices may work back and forth in a small or large range, but over such a brief period of time that the moving average indicators are almost constantly out of phase with market activity. In such cases, the moving average system will not fare well, and indeed, it may fare worse than most systems. However, in a trending market, moving average systems shine.

## OSCILLATORS

I remember once watching a footrace between two college athletes. The race distance was one lap of a quarter-mile cinder track. At the start, both racers were staying close, with one (red socks) seemingly setting the pace for the other (yellow socks). As they completed approximately one-third of the race, however, red socks began pulling away, lengthening the distance between himself and yellow socks. It seemed he would surely win the race. But then, as they started into the third corner of the track, red socks began to falter, and yellow socks began to gain on him. On the fourth corner, they were again neck and neck, but yellow socks was moving faster and soon passed him. In the final stretch, yellow socks continued to increase the distance between them in a strong finish. red socks, nearly exhausted, stumbled across the finish line and stopped, breathing heavily, holding his sides.

A market trend is very similar to the runner I have dubbed red socks. In the early stages of the trend, prices move steadily in the direction of the trend. As the trend continues, prices begin to move more rapidly, as more trades jump into the market. But then, prices lose their momentum and begin to move more slowly until, finally, exhausted, they stop moving in that direction altogether and change direction.

If a trader can know when prices are losing their momentum, he might have a good idea that the present trend is about to reverse itself. In the race I watched, it was easy to see the difference between the two runners expand and contract. If that difference were measured each 30 seconds, and the measurements were plotted on a graph, the result would look like Figure 8-27. Keep in mind that we are only measuring the difference between the runners, not the speed at which they are running.

Early in the race, with red socks leading, the difference was small, perhaps five feet, but positive. During this time, both runners may have increased their speed, but the critical measurement was the distance between them, which remained constant. Later, as red socks pulled away, the distance increased, forming a rising line on the chart. As the distance between the runners increases more rapidly, the line on the chart moves up more steeply. A steeper line indicates greater momentum of change. We still do not care about the actual speed of the runners.

Finally, as yellow socks overtakes and passes red socks, the line plotting the difference between them moves down toward zero, crosses zero, and becomes an increasingly large negative value. By plotting the changing distance between the two runners, we have illustrated

*Figure 8–27.   Diagram of Footrace Oscillator.*

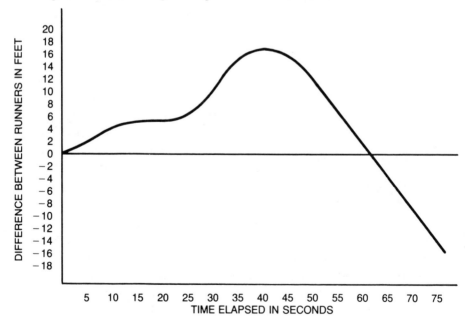

the momentum of that changing distance. By watching a real-time plot of the changing distance, we would know precisely the completion of the race from start to finish, without watching the race itself.

The diagram we have constructed from this footrace can be called a momentum line. It measures the rate, or the momentum, of change. The farthest distance that could occur between the runners is the length of the track. If we assign that distance a value of +1 or −1 on the chart, with the zero line in the middle, we have created a momentum oscillator.

In the market a similar phenomenon can be obtained by subtracting a price $x$ days ago from today's price and plotting the value obtained on a graph. If the price $x$ days ago is greater than the current price, the value will be negative, and if the price $x$ days ago is less than the current price, the value will be positive. When these values are plotted, they form a curving line that moves around a zero line, as in Figure 8-28. When the difference between the prices is the same for several days, the line will be straight. As the difference increases, the line moves up. As the difference decreases, the line moves down. This is the measure of momentum, or the rate of change, in prices. This measure of momentum of change can be normalized, just as we did for the chart of the two runners. At that point, we have a momentum *oscillator.*

This is the most fundamental of the various kinds of oscillators that are used by market analysts. All oscillators tend to look alike on a chart. They consist of a band across the bottom of the chart, with a line that fluctuates, or oscillates, above and below a midpoint. Some oscillators use a zero midpoint, with +1 and −1 representing the boundaries. Others use a scale from zero to 100. Whatever form they take, oscillators are designed to measure the underlying strength of a price move in the market.

Oscillators are normally used in conjunction with other trend-following analysis tools and subordinated to

*Figure 8–28. Daily Oscillator.*

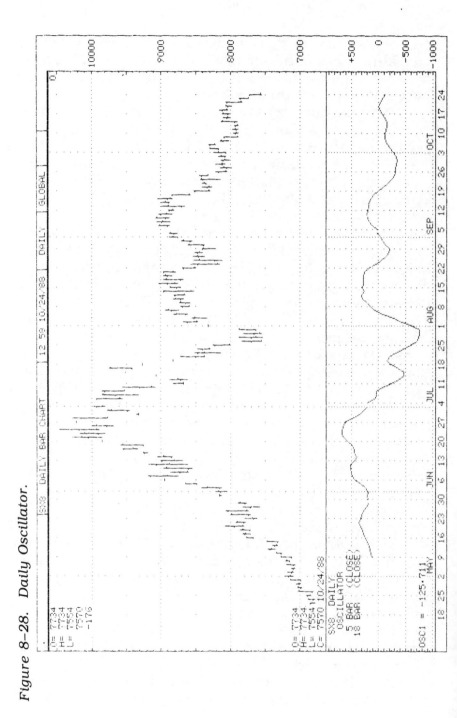

them. They are rarely used alone. Although valuable in trending markets, oscillators are particularly useful in nontrending markets, where prices are fluctuating within a price bond, commonly called a *trading range*.

A momentum oscillator is helpful in alerting the trader to an overbought or oversold market condition. When the oscillator reaches the extremes of the chart, it may indicate that the price move has gone too far too fast, just as our tired runner, and is due to change direction. A momentum oscillator is useful in three ways. First, it provides overbought and oversold signals, as we just mentioned. Second, as the oscillator crosses the zero line, it gives buy or sell signals. To understand why, remember our runners. When yellow socks overtook and passed red socks, it became more likely that he would win the race. That is when the oscillator, which was plotting the completion of the race, crossed the zero line. The third function of a momentum oscillator is to measure divergence. When the direction of price is different from the direction of the oscillator, this can be a particularly strong signal.

Momentum oscillators can be very helpful tools for a trader to use. However, they suffer from some significant shortcomings. First, momentum oscillators tend to be very erratic because they are subject to extreme price moves on either side of the calculation. Second, momentum oscillators lack a standardized upper and lower boundary applicable to all markets. These two weaknesses have made the momentum oscillator difficult to work with and have led to the development of more sophisticated and useful oscillators.

*Relative Strength Index*

By using the average of the up closes and the average of the down closes for a 14-day period and fitting them into a formula, Welles Wilder has constructed an oscillator that can identify overbought and oversold conditions on a standard scale of zero to 100, applicable to any market. His *relative strength index* (RSI) solved the dual problems of erratic movement and a lack of constant boundaries. As a result, this index has become very popular with technical analysts, and it appears on the charts from numerous chart services and market quote services.

On the RSI, the 70 and 30 lines represent the boundaries for overbought and oversold conditions, respectively. Theoretically, when the RSI oscillator goes above 70, the market is not able to maintain its current level of strength and is due for a reversal. The converse is true of the 30 line. As with the momentum oscillator, the highs and lows of the RSI precede market tops and bottoms, making it a leading indicator.

Some analysts find the 70-30 lines to be too sensitive and choose instead to work on 80-20. The bands chosen must be selected with care, in order with 75-25 to balance the need to identify more trading opportunities against entering the market too soon. As with most market tools, the individual trader will fit it to his or her particular style of trading. The ultimate test of the effectiveness of any market analysis tool is its profitability in the market.

The RSI provides, in addition to overbought and oversold signals, various chart formations, just as the bar chart itself did. As the trader watches the RSI, he might notice a failure swing or a double top or bottom (Figure 8-29). Support and resistance areas can also be found. A very important characteristic of the RSI, however, is divergence from price action (Figure 8-30). When the RSI is in an overbought or oversold area, and the oscillator is moving in a direction opposite that of the price, this is a very strong indicator of a turning point in the market.

### Stochastics

A curious phenomenon often occurs in the futures market. As prices increase, the closing price is usually closer to the upper end of the price bar, and as prices

*Figure 8–29. RSI Showing Failure Swing/Double Top or Bottom.*

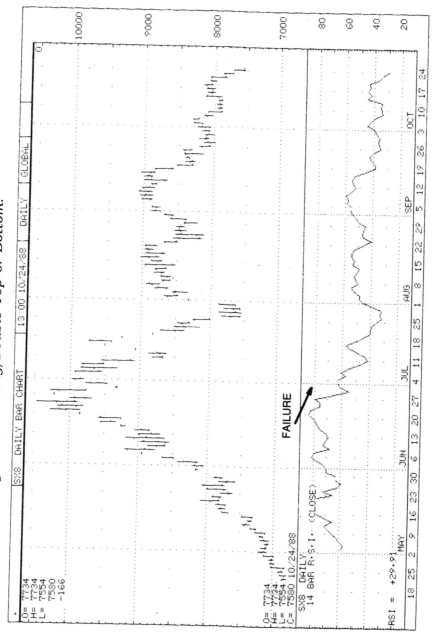

*Figure 8–30. RSI Divergence from Price Direction.*

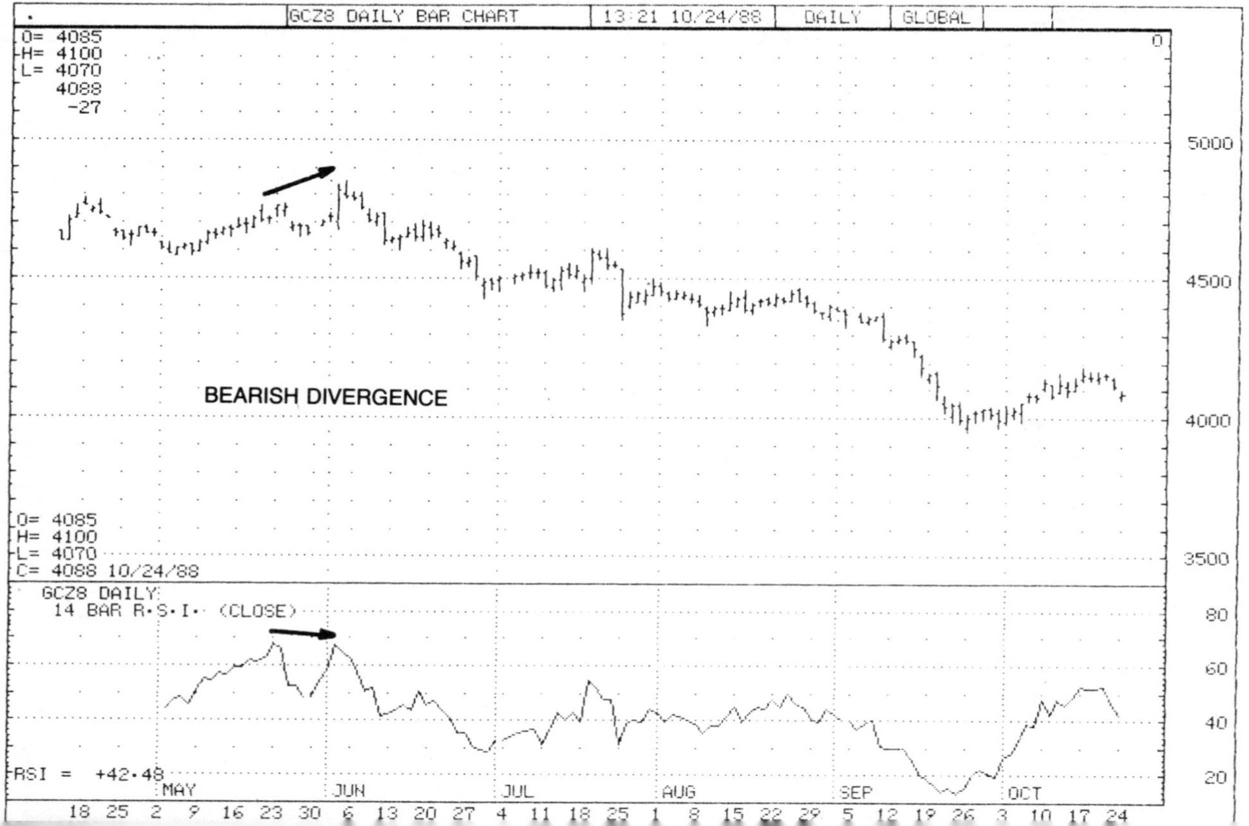

decrease, the closing price is usually closer to the lower end of the price bar. This phenomenon is curious only because of its consistency, not because it is unexpected.

As I have said so often, the chart of a market is really a diagram of the behavior of the players in the market. Therefore, in a bull market, the buyers are stronger than the sellers and tend to push prices up toward the end of the day, while in a bear market the converse is true. Toward the end of a trend, however, as the pressure that has supported the trend weakens, a new pattern develops. In a bull market, buying pressure weakens as a reversal approaches. The result is that prices continue to hit new highs, but the closing price moves closer to the low end of the price bar, or the low price of the day. A bear market reversal will see a similar pattern in reverse.

*Stochastics* is simply an oscillator that measures the relative position of the closing price within the price bar, or the daily price range, and uses that information to forecast a market turn. Most quote systems offer stochastics, and many chart services carry the stochastic graph at the bottom of the chart.

The mathematical calculations involved in stochastics are too complex for the scope of this book, but the pattern looks like a double oscillator. The slow line, which is called %D, is a three-day moving average of the faster line, which is called %K. As the %K line crosses %D, market signals are given. With stochastics, significant signals results from left and right crossovers (Figure 8-31), extreme turns, and reduction of speed.

### Other Oscillators

Larry Williams has become well known in recent years for his performance in the Robbins Trading Company World Cup Championship of Futures Trading. His trading in that competition was based on oscillator systems he has been developing and refining for many years. In 1972 he published a description of his A/D oscillator.

*Figure 8-31.* Stochastic Indicator.

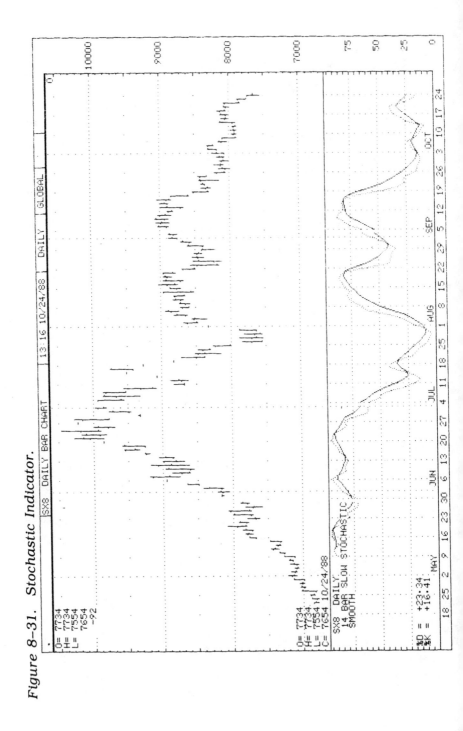

This was followed by the %R oscillator, which is really a 10-day stochastic. Most recently, he has developed what he calls the ultimate oscillator, which seems to combine the original A/D oscillator with Wilder's RSI.

Another variation of the use of oscillators is the Cambridge Hook, developed by Dr. James Kneafsey. This system combines an outside reversal day (a higher high followed by a lower close) with Wilder's RSI and a measure of volume and open interest. When all three conditions are met, the signal is very accurate in predicting trend reversals.

## VOLUME AND OPEN INTEREST

Most technical analysts do not make decisions based on only one or two pieces of information. Some market information is of a primary nature—that is, distinct market signals are communicated. Price is a primary market indicator.

Other information is of a secondary nature. It is used to substantiate or confirm the primary signals. *Volume* and *open interest* are secondary indicators, but they are very significant to many traders. Many persons new to futures trading are confused by the concepts of volume and open interest. Once you understand the distinction, however, you will also understand the significance of each.

Volume is the total number of contracts traded on a given day. To find the volume, add the total of the short positions taken that day, *or* add the total of the long positions taken that day. Do *not* add the two together. (Remember, a contract requires a buyer and a seller.)

Open interest is the total number of contracts still outstanding at the end of a given day. To find the open interest in a market, add the number of short positions still being held at the close of the trading day, *or* add the total number of long positions being held at the end of the day. Do *not* add the two together.

Even though there is a dearth of research regarding the relationship of volume and open interest to the market, most market analysts watch both statistics closely, along with price. Newspaper price charts carry the volume and open interest figures on a daily basis, which makes it relatively easy to use these data even without sophisticated market quote systems.

The common wisdom among traders and analysts is that price, volume, and open interest have the following relationship, as shown in Table 8-1.

Generally, rising prices combined with declining volume and open interest are seen as a signal for a price reversal. When volume and open interest are both increasing, the common thinking is that the present trend will continue because open interest tends to increase during a trending period.

## THE WAVE THEORIES

Anyone with more than a casual acquaintance with stocks or commodities has likely heard of the *Elliott wave*. Developed by R. N. Elliott in the late 1920s and early 1930s, the Elliott wave is related to the theories

TABLE 8-1. VOLUME AND OPEN INTEREST INTERPRETATION.

| Price | Volume | Open Interest | Market |
|---|---|---|---|
| Increasing | Increasing | Increasing | Technically strong |
| Increasing | Decreasing | Decreasing | Technically weak |
| Decreasing | Increasing | Increasing | Technically weak |
| Decreasing | Decreasing | Decreasing | Technically strong |

of stock market behavior that were first published by Charles H. Dow.

In a series of editorials in the *Wall Street Journal* around the turn of the century, Dow proposed several basic principles regarding the stock market averages that he had established and that still bear his name. These theoretical rules are precursors of much of the technical analysis that has been covered in this chapter.

Dow's theory first established the concept that all fundamental supply and demand factors that affect the market are assimilated into the price action. He went on to draw an analogy between the behavior of market prices and the ocean. He described the primary price trend in terms of the tide, while secondary trends are like the waves that follow the tide successfully higher onto the beach. Minor trends are the ripples in the waves. He noted that secondary trends, which are retracements of the primary trend, usually recede approximately one-third to two-thirds of the distance covered by the primary trend. These corrections are often close to 50%. Dow further postulated that each major trend has three distinct phases: an accumulation period, a period of rapidly enhancing prices and improving business news, and the final period during which economic news is rosy and volume increases markedly as the public begins to participate actively in the market.

Elliott adopted Dow's comparison between the ocean and the stock market in his scholarly extension of this pioneering work. In Elliott's original theoretical treatises, and in the work that has expanded and refined Elliott's principles, we find five waves within major bull markets ("tidal wave" bull markets). Each of these five waves can be divided into five subwaves. (see Figure 8-32). In the correction phase, each move involves three waves, which can also be divided into three subwaves.

Although based on elegantly simple precepts, Elliott's wave theory is quite complex and difficult to utilize in market trading. Anyone wishing to apply wave theory to a trading program would be well advised to study

*Figure 8-32.  Elliott Wave Showing Five Up/Three Down.*

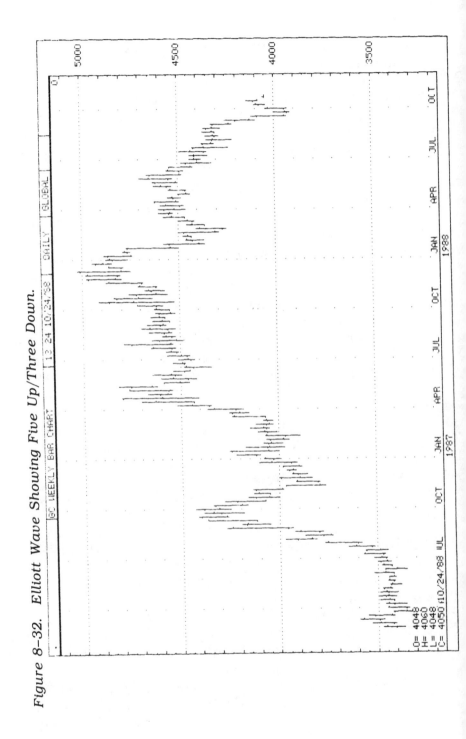

thoroughly the original material by Elliott, as well as the expansion of that work done by A. H. Bolton. The most recent and probably the most thorough analysis and application of Elliott's theories has been done by Robert Prechter.


## FIBONACCI NUMBER SERIES

Dow first noted that retracements of price waves were often 50% of the original wave, with the range extending from one-third to two-thirds. Elliott, in carrying Dow's work further, based his own wave theories on a series of similar percentage relationships or ratios that have their roots in ancient Egyptian and Greek civilizations. The Egyptians used a ratio of 0.618 or 1.618 in their construction of the Great Pyramid of Giza. The ratio of the elevation to the base is 0.618, a ratio that the Egyptians called the golden ratio. The Greeks applied this same ratio, which they called the golden mean, to the construction of the Parthenon.

It was left to a relatively unknown 13th-century Italian mathematician named Leonardo Fibonacci, however, to discover these mathematical ratios and, by so doing, give his name to a number series that seems to be elemental to much of the physical and metaphysical world in which we live. Having observed and studied the Great Pyramid, Fibonacci carried the numerical relationships further when he studied the mathematical problem of the reproduction of rabbits.

Having established the basic conditions that every month a pair of rabbits produces a new pair of rabbits, which then become reproductive from the second month on, producing new pairs at the same rate, without any deaths occurring, Fibonacci developed his "summation series":

1, 1, 2, 3, 5, 8, 13, 21, 34, 55, 89, 144 . . .

At first glance, this number series seems to be only a random grouping of numbers. The relationship becomes clear, however, when you discover that each number in the series is the sum of the previous two numbers. Moreover, the ratio of each consecutive pair of numbers approaches 0.618 or 1.618 after the first four numbers: $1/2 = 0.50$; $2/3 = 0.667$; $8/13 = 0.615$; $35/34 = 1.618$. These numbers and ratios seem to occur throughout the natural world: in the sunflower, in the chambered nautilus, in a musical octave (eight white keys and five black, totaling 13), and in the artistic works of Leonardo da Vinci.

By applying these *Fibonacci ratios* to the stock market, Elliott discovered that these mathematical relationships could be observed there as well. It is fascinating to think that market prices—which, as we have said, reflect the behavior of human psychology—would follow patterns of activity so closely related to seemingly elemental relationships that exist throughout nature. And yet, as Elliott has demonstrated, the ratios of the various waves and retracement waves often fall very closely within the Fibonacci ratios of 0.50, 0.618, and 1.618.

# CHAPTER 9

# The Psychology of Investing

When I set out to write this book, my purpose was very clear: to provide a comprehensive yet concise introduction to futures trading and the complex and esoteric world of commodity futures and options. After having covered the historical development of a futures contract, the scope of the futures market, the nitty-gritty of futures trading, the proliferation of technology with which to analyze the markets both from a technical and a fundamental point of view, the use of options on futures as an alternative investment strategy, and the nature of speculation in a free market economy, the temptation is to consider the job now finished. In fact, if I believed the common wisdom taught by the majority of brokerage houses and futures trading advisors in the industry, I indeed would need to write no more of this book. Most such experts would have us believe that knowledge of the markets is the key to speculative profit. The catch-word among these investment strategists has been for some time *market knowledge.* "Discounts save money—knowledge makes money," asserts one brokerage house.

But if I were to lay down my pen now, having provided you with only the mechanical and technological aspects of futures trading, I would have left out the most important component in the futures trading equation—the trader. In the 16th century, Michel de Montaigne cautioned us that "we can be knowledgeable with other men's knowledge, but we cannot be wise with other men's wisdom." I have thus far attempted to impart the knowledge necessary to an understanding of the futures industry. The purpose of this chapter is to help the reader understand the wisdom that separates successful traders from mediocre and worse ones. I will not attempt to teach wisdom—only the path to market wisdom and self-knowledge. I will teach you how to analyze the differences between two traders—one successful, one not—who use identical information and systems. In short, I will try to teach you the psychology of successful investing.

## THE PARADOX

The past several decades of technological development have rendered an interesting paradox in the world of commodity investing. With computerized systems and lightning-fast communication and advanced economic forecasting, there should be an overwhelming number of market winners. Which of you did not have the feeling, as you read the chapter on technical analysis, that "this is easy; I can take these systems and be very successful"? But why should you be, when over 90% of all investors in commodity futures trading are unsuccessful? Why are less than 10% successful? The answers to these questions lie with the individual trader, for it is the individual who stands in his or her own way when it comes to prospering as a trader. The speculator who takes sophisticated market tools and uses them to create losses rather than gains can only look to his or her own limitations. The average investor who feeds the market with losses can blame only a lack of self-knowledge, self-control, and self-discipline.

In spite of overwhelming technological knowledge, the paradox is that most traders still lose money in the futures market. The limiting factor in a highly complex system continues to be the human being, who seems to have removed himself or herself from the situation he or she sought to improve through technology. The fact is that knowledge of one's self seems to be more important than the acquisition of so-called facts, news, economic theories, or political motivations. The markets of the 1980s and 1990s will continue to be unstable and unpredictable, as opposed to the 1950s and 1960s. It is therefore essential that any speculator hoping to be successful in such a chaotic marketplace have a command of his or her emotional self.

In the chapter on technical analysis, the point was made that chart patterns are little more than a diagram of market psychology. Thus, the various trend lines, reversal patterns, and support and resistance points on a bar chart have no direct relationship to the commodity itself, but rather they reflect the attempts by market traders to cope with forces inside themselves. The rising and falling value of the commodity is a function of what buyers and sellers at any one time and place are willing to pay or receive for it. (Remember the discussion of supply and demand and elasticity of supply and demand?) The final act of buying and selling in a marketplace must be performed by people who have examined the situation, considered the variables, studied the charts, and arrived at their conclusions. The information available for study is the same for everyone, yet the conclusions can be worlds apart. The explanation for this phenomenon may lie with Francis Bacon's observation: "Man prefers to believe what he prefers to be true."

What a trader prefers to be true is a function of that trader's inner psychological state. Therefore, a study of the theories and principles of human psychology and human behavior are just as important—if not more so— than an understanding of market fundamentals, trading systems, chart analysis, and economic theory, for it is human behavior that causes market behavior.

## BASIC HUMAN PSYCHOLOGY

Human behavior can be studied from a number of perspectives. Indeed, there are many different psychological theories and schools of thought—so many as to be quite confusing to the individual desiring a basic understanding of human behavior. To simplify the situation, most, if not all schools of thought, can be categorized under two broad classifications. Just as there are fundamental analysts and technical analysts in the marketplace, so there are fundamental psychological theories that grow out of the belief that human developmental factors cause later behavior patterns, and there are opposing technical (behavioral) theories that state that human behavior is simply a learned response to environmental elements.

Of course, numerous market analysts take an eclectic approach, combining fundamental with technical theories in an attempt to utilize as much information as possible in the decision-making process. So, too, are there eclectic practitioners in the field of psychology.

The traditional psychologist, with his or her roots in Freudian psychology, studies the underlying causes of human behavior. This psychologist asks questions like these:

* Why do people act the way they do?

* What are the underlying causes of behavior and mental disturbance?

* How can we use the life history of an individual to help him or her?

* What motivates people to act in certain ways?

* What are the sexual and unconscious processes that stimulate behavior?

These questions, as we can see, are very much like those asked by a market fundamentalist. Both are searching for the *why* of behavior—one is looking at market behavior; the other is looking at human behavior.

The behavioral psychologist is quite similar to the technical analyst. His or her orientation is simply the measurement of overt behavior and the establishing of identifiable patterns. The questions asked by a behavioral psychologist are these:

* How often does a certain behavior occur?

* What are the events that maintain behavior?

* What happens before and after a given behavior?

* Can the behavior be changed by manipulation of environmental conditions?

* How long does it take to change behavior using certain methods?

* How long has the current behavior been present?

Questions of this nature lead to behavioral study that is essentially technical. Just as the technical market analyst employs specific trend determination and measurement methods, so does the behavioral psychologist measure behavior trends and the frequency of behavior patterns.

Self-understanding and self-awareness can come via both schools of thought, just as the market can be understood more clearly with both a broad grasp of the fundamental forces that act on commodity prices and a keen study of the recurring patterns of price behavior. Taking steps to change undesirable behavior, however, can often be quicker and more effective when done systematically, according to the princples of behavioral psychology. So, too, can trading decisions be made more quickly and with a keener sense of timing when using a technical system for analyzing the market. This is why fundamental analysts tend to be longer-term position traders while technical analysts tend to "daytrade" or hold other short-term positions.

### Psychoanalytic Theory

Traditional psychoanalysts attribute human behavior to unconscious motivation born out of basic childhood developmental stages and the success or failure of the individual to pass through and adjust to each stage in a healthful manner. Freud identified four stages of development: (1) the oral stage, during which the baby experiences the world through oral activities such as biting, licking, and tasting—this stage generally continues through the first year of life; (2) the anal stage, during which behavior centers around the child's eliminative habits and the struggle between parent and child regarding that issue; (3) the genital stage and the discovery both of sexual pleasure and the differentiation of the sexes; (4) the latency period, which leads to the development of "defense mechanisms." Problems in any of the developmental stages, which, by the way, are not remembered later in life, can cause behavioral aberrations in the adult. Psychoanalysis seeks to discover the developmental circumstances that may have led to adult behavior problems.

A cornerstone of psychoanalytic theory is the concept of defense mechanisms. As a source of understanding the behavior of others and ourselves, these protective attitudes and actions, designed to defend the individual from childhood memories and experiences too painful or threatening to remember, can be very helpful. Among the more well-known and studied are these:

* *Sublimation* is the process of refining childhood impulses into socially acceptable behavior.

* *Castration complex/Oedipal complex* are concepts that describe the struggle of the child, who fears punishment in the form of castration and is therefore sexually attracted to the parent of the opposite sex.

* *Repression* is the process whereby early childhood experiences or later traumatic events are forgotten or thrown into the subconscious.

* *Suppression* is an intentional act of repression, as opposed to the otherwise unconscious nature of repression.

* *Regression* refers to a tendency to resort to child-like behavior.

* *Reaction-formation* is an unusually strong dislike that occurs as the result of a similar behavior as a child, which, of course, has been forgotten or repressed.

* *Intellectualization,* or *rationalization,* is a very common self-protective behavior that attempts to explain problematic behavior through what appears to be logic and common sense.

*Learning Theory*

Whereas the traditional "fundamental" psychologist wants to know what went wrong in childhood development that causes aberrant behavior in the adult, the learning theorist, or behavioral theorist, looks simply at the behavior itself and what might be causing it or maintaining it. This school of thought dates back to the 1920s and the Russian physiologist I. P. Pavlov, who studied the salivary reflexes of dogs. He demonstrated that various responses could be conditioned to arousal by stimuli that were not originally related to the response itself. In these now classic experiments, Pavlov combined a bell or a buzzer with the presentation of food, and by so doing he taught the dogs to salivate at the sound of the bell or the buzzer, even when there was no food present.

Later in the experiment, as the sounds continued to be presented without any accompanying food, however, the salivation slowed and eventually stopped, in a process now known as *extinction.* The process of teaching the dogs to salivate at the sound of a bell is known as *reflexive conditioning.* Researchers have discovered that virtually any behavior can be taught to humans or animals through this kind of basic conditioning. Thus, a behavioral psychologist presented with an irrational fear or a disturbing behavior by a client either would search for the environmental circumstance that had conditioned the behavior and try to eliminate it (extinction) or would attempt to condition a new behavior to replace the disturbing one.

The learning paradigm, according to the behaviorist, is this: Something in the environment acts on the organism, which then responds, eliciting any of a number of consequences. If the consequence is pleasurable, the behavior will be more likely to reoccur, and the consequence is said to be reinforcing. If, however, the consequence is negative, the behavior will be more likely to cease. Thus, the behaviorist, like the market technician, is in a position simply to chart the behavior under various conditions in order to determine a possible treatment. There is no need to look for the fundamental childhood experiences that might have caused the behavior. Figure 9-1 represents the paradigm of behavioral learning.

FIGURE 9-1.  THE LEARNING PARADIGM.

| Environment→Stimulus→Organism→Response(s)→Consequence(s) |
| --- |

Source: *The Investor's Quotient.*

## THE APPLICATION OF LEARNING THEORY TO COMMODITY TRADING

In the futures market, if conditions were ideal, the learning paradigm outlined in Figure 9-1 should lead to the development of an excellent trading record. Let's assume that a market trader has chosen, from among the technical systems outlined in Chapter 8, a trading system of some validity and accuracy, of which there are many. As this system provides various buy-and-sell signals, the trader responds by either buying or selling or doing nothing. As a consequence of that behavior, the trader experiences a profit, a loss, or no economic change if the choice was to do nothing. Theoretically, if the consequence is a profit, which is pleasurable, the action taken will have been reinforced and is more likely to reoccur. Conversely, if the consequence is a loss, the action is less likely to be repeated. The consequence for no action might be pleasurable or not, depending on what would have happened if action had been taken. Figure 9-2 is a representation of this sequence of events.

It is easy to see with this figure that a good technical system should lead to a profitable trading record by rewarding good decisions and punishing wrong decisions. Unfortunately, such a perfect state of events rarely occurs. At each stage of the paradigm, many things can go wrong, and often do. Take, for example, the following

FIGURE 9-2.  THE INVESTOR AND THE LEARNING PARADIGM.

| Stimulus | Organism | Response | Consequences |
|---|---|---|---|
| Markets Signals Indicators | Speculator Trader | Buy or sell Do nothing | Profit/loss |
| #1 | #2 | #3 | #4 |

Source: *The Investor's Quotient.*

case from my book *The Investor's Quotient* (Wiley, New York, 1980), which illustrates what can happen at stage #1.

A certain trader follows commodities on the basis of moving averages. Each time the three moving averages he monitors are moving up or when one important average crosses the other, a signal to buy is flashed. The appropriate response would be to buy. Let us assume, however, that the trader has just finished reading the *Wall Street Journal*. The lead article discusses several bearish factors in pork bellies. The trader then turns to his chart, which clearly signals "buy bellies." He is presented with two sets of conflicting information. On the one hand, experts who wrote the article claim that prices will move lower; on the other hand, his signals say that the market will go up. What should he do? His dilemma is not unlike one experienced by all of us at some time or another.

If the market signals or indicators are unclear or conflicting, the trader can easily become confused and take the wrong action, with the result that faulty reasoning will take place. Whatever the consequence of the action may be, it will obviously follow an incorrect or inconsistent behavior, and its impact on that behavior will be meaningless at best and will encourage inconsistent behavior at worst.

Let's look at some possible outcomes. Assume first that the trader follows his technical signal. This, of course, would be the best thing to do. The net result might be a profit. This has been a learning experience with positive consequences. He or she has not only been rewarded for following the system but has also been rewarded for not being influenced by another source of information. Whether the contradictory information came from the news media, a broker, a friend, or an advisory service, the mere fact that this trader followed his or her own system was a great achievement. Only several such positive events are necessary for the behavior to be stamped in, or learned. Unfortunately, most traders never pass step one. Their very first trades often are not a result of a system but follow outside influences unrelated to the system. Their system, whether intrinsically good or bad, never has the opportunity to be tested. Hence, learning is faulty from the start.

Let's assume that our trader does not follow his signal but rather takes advice given by a report, a broker, or a friend. And let's assume additionally that his or her original signal would have been wrong and a loss would have resulted. By avoiding the negative experience of a loss, the trader has been rewarded for behavior that will not only be difficult to eliminate later but will also prevent the trading system from being tested in real time. The probability is that this individual will act similarly in the future. Thus, the system may never get tested, and, in fact, it will most likely be abandoned completely.

Let us assume a third possible outcome. The trader follows his or her signal and takes a loss. A negative experience resulted from following a signal. Paradoxically, the negative result will eventually have a positive effect. By repeatedly following a signal, our trader will test the system in actual markets and thereby learn if the signal is good or bad. Without consistent use of the signal, there will be no learning.

Of even greater importance in this situation is the concept of partial or random reinforcement. Let's assume that our trader follows some signals and not others. Let's also assume that some of the trades made by this individual are recommended by brokers, advisory services, or similar agents. Essentially, this individual is on a schedule of reinforcement in which his or her behavior—selecting a trade—is not linked to any one stimulus. This confounds the learning process and leaves the individual not only poorly trained but also in a state of insecurity and confusion.

The second aspect of partial reinforcement relates to the "addictive" nature of speculation and, for that matter, all forms of gambling. There is enough variability in the market to provide most traders with partial or random rewards. This schedule will result in a strong attachment to the market, making the trading habit difficult to break. Whatever that outcome, the number of random wins will act toward the creation of a very strong bond between trader and market. Thousands of traders who have been maintained on a random schedule by the market may fit into this category. For every one winning trade there may be 10 losers. And yet, the game goes on and the losses continue. Now imagine the individual who does not stick to one specific trading plan. The combined effect of partial reinforcement from acceptance of signals and trades from other sources can create a confused, frustrated, addicted loser. It is thus easy to see how things can go wrong at stage #1 and lead to poor trading performance. Stage #2, however, is also fraught with danger.

If the stimulus at stage #1 is not mixed or confusing but is very clear, then the potential for learning from faulty behavior now lies with the trader. The greatest risk at this stage is screening the market signal, which results in indecision. Rather than simply perceiving the signal and carrying out the trade, the trader engages in "what-if" behavior, or waits a while to verify the signal, or checks some other sources to see whether or not they agree with the signal. In this case, faulty behavior is again likely to occur as the trader screens the signal through his or her own perceptual filter, either taking no action through lack of confidence or taking the wrong action through second-guessing the system. See Figure 9-3 for a diagram of this process.

The third stage of the learning paradigm is response. We have seen how the stimulus (the trading signal) can be confusing at stage #1, and we have seen how the trader can filter the signal at stage #2, resulting in inappropriate action. At stage #3, there is still the potential for faulty reasoning to take place. Many inexperienced traders (and far too many veterans, unfortunately) attempt the correct response to a clear market signal only to find the trade doesn't work because of a technically

FIGURE 9-3.   TRADING PARADIGM AND PERCEPTUAL FILTER.

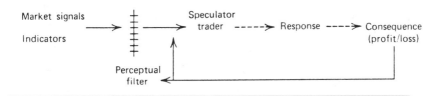

Source: *Investor's Quotient.*

incorrect response. Typical of this situation is the trader who, after receiving a buy signal, places an order to buy at the market rather than at a specified price, only to find that the order was filled a long way from the intended price, thus eroding any potential profit. Another common error is the placement of a stop-loss order too close to the entry point. How frustrating it is to watch the market move down, take out a stop, and then move in the intended direction, leaving the trader with a loss rather than a significant profit.

There are, of course, a multitude of technical errors that can be made in spite of a trader's best intentions, resulting in inconsistent consequences (stage #4) and faulty reasoning. The clear message is that the would-be trader should become proficient at the technical process of trading in the market, in addition to paying attention to the development of a good trading system.

The final stage of the learning paradigm is the consequence of the behavioral response. To understand what can go wrong at stage #4, I refer again to *The Investor's Quotient.* It is natural to assume that a profit will tend to increase a trader's use of profitable signals, whereas a loss will tend to decrease use of such signals. But this is not always the way it works. The behavioral definition of the term "reinforcement" (reward) considers a reinforcer to be anything that increases the frequency of a given behavior. This makes it possible for an event or circumstance that is seen as negative to act as a reinforcer. For example, a classic study on classroom behavior revealed that children who were scolded by a teacher for out-of-seat behavior tended to exhibit more of this behavior than children who were ignored. In other words, the "punishment" the teachers thought they were administering was actually functioning as positive reinforcement. It was possible to determine that this was happening by measuring the increase or decrease in out-of-seat behavior.

If you have ever punished children or pets only to find that they are misbehaving even more than before the punishment was started, then you know how "punishment" can act as a reward. In fact, punishment is a form of attention, and to some individuals negative attention acts as a reward. The causes of such peculiarity can also be explained in behavioral terms. Suffice it to say, however, that the ultimate value of anything considered a reward must be measured in terms of its effect. If I believe that I am rewarding someone for a given behavior, and if the behavior does not increase in frequency, then I am not truly rewarding it. Another reinforcer must be found. If I believe that I am punishing a given behavior and see it increase in frequency, then indeed I am not punishing it and must look for another punishment.

I am reminded of the individual who called me one day seeking consultation on his trading. Asked to precisely define the problem, he stated, "I just can't make any money in the market. Every trade I make turns into a loss. Every time I put in a stop it's hit. Every time I meet a margin call I get still another. And all my friends think I'm an ass." The following conversation between us revealed the reasons for his trading decisions:

> "How do you feel when you lose?" I asked.
> "Bad," he replied without hesitation.
> "How bad?" I probed.
> "I feel so bad that I can hardly get home from the office," he responded.
> "How do you get home?" I questioned further.
> "My friends drive me."

"Do you go straight home?"

"Well, not really. First we stop and have a few stiff belts at the local bar. That helps me forget about my losses. Then we have dinner at a good restaurant."

"What then?" I asked.

"Then I go home and tell my wife about how badly the market's punished me."

"And what does she do?"

"She gets all hysterical. She tells me that she's going to get a divorce if I keep losing money in the market. She has tantrums and throws things at me. Then she calls her mother. And her mother gets hysterical, too. Sometimes her mother comes over and throws things at me, too. It's almost funny to see how upset the two of them get. It's as if they had earned the money I lost."

"And how do you feel when they get upset?" I asked.

"Well, like I said, it's almost funny, if you know what I mean. I kind of enjoy watching those two shrews frothing at the mouth . . . serves them right."

"What is it about them getting upset that seems funny?"

"Well, all these years I've been working and slaving at my business while the two of them spend my money. I wish she'd honor her threat and divorce me. Then I could do anything I wanted to do. I could stay out late, not come home at all if I don't want to, go fishing when I want to, and trade the market as much as I want. If I didn't have to worry about her big mouth, then I could make money in the market. I feel good when she gets mad. I'll show her who's boss . . . who makes all the money . . . and if I want to lose in the market, then I'll lose it in the market . . . it's my money!"

"Sounds to me like you really enjoy getting your wife upset," I observed.

"Wouldn't you enjoy it, too, if your wife was a nagging bitch like mine is? Wouldn't you want to get her mad and make her suffer, too?" he pleaded.

"Sounds to me like you enjoy getting your wife upset more than you dread the pain of losing money in the market. In fact, it seems as if you lose in the market with the intention of getting her so upset that she'll eventually divorce you. The market is merely a tool for you. You're using it to get something that's much more important to you than either profits or losses," I noted further.

"That's the biggest bunch of bull I've ever heard," he commented as he left.

Several years later I had the good fortune to meet him at a commodity seminar. He apologized for his behavior on the telephone and told me that my original observation of his problem was correct. After going through a bankruptcy, a divorce, and several hundred thousand dollars in market losses, he was forced to stop trading. During his involuntary retirement from the market, he realized the stimulus-response consequence of his behavior. He explained it to me as follows:

"The problem with my trading was not really related to my trading at all. When I first started in the market, I took some losses the way all traders do. But each time I took a loss, I would make a big deal about it. I complained to my friends and business partners. They felt sorry for me. And I wanted them to. Every time I took a loss, they'd try to cheer me up. I enjoyed the attention. Instead of taking the loss, forgetting about it, and moving on to the next trade, I milked it for all the attention I could get. I had a nagging feeling after a while that I might be losing on purpose. But it was hard to accept that possibility. All I know is that every time I took a loss, I got a great deal of attention. I'd tell my friends about the big profit I took and they'd say, 'That's great, Chuck, old boy, I knew you could do it.' And that was it. Whenever I took a profit, they made no special deal about it. Possibly, they were jealous. But when I was a loser, it was somehow an occasion to celebrate. We'd go out and drink under the guise of 'drowning the loss.' I realize now that this was acting as a reward for losing. I should have received absolutely no attention for being a loser. We should have gone out partying when I had made a profit. The money wasn't nearly as important a reward as was the attention."

"And to make things even worse, the losses upset my family. My wife would punish me. But all the time she didn't realize that I enjoyed her being aggravated. I didn't realize it either. The consequences of my losing were serving some very important purposes in my life. Not only did they get me attention from friends, but they also irritated my wife. And that made me happy. If I had realized the connection between losses and their consequences, I might have been able to change the outcome. I realize it now. Fortunately, it's not too late."

I asked him how his trading was going. "Couldn't be much better," he replied proudly. "I know now that the market is much less important than me. I know that every loss is a lesson and every profit is a reward. Each time I lose, I forget about it as soon as I can. I try to see if I made a mistake in reading my trading system. If I made a mistake, then I write it down and keep a record of it. I consult it often to make certain that I don't make the same mistakes repeatedly. When I take a loss, it's just between me and my broker. I mention it to no one else. When I take a profit, I celebrate. I spend some of the money, put some in the bank, and tell my friends about how smart I am. I pat myself on the back and enjoy all the rewards that the profit should bring."

## EVALUATING UNPRODUCTIVE OR UNSUCCESSFUL TRADING

At the beginning of this chapter, I promised to teach you how to analyze the differences between two traders who may use the same information and follow the same technical systems, yet who experience widely different levels of success. The four stages of the learning paradigm provide the mechanics for that analysis. Any trader who does consistently well, any trader who does consistently poorly, and any trader who is inconsistent in his results can look for understanding regarding his performance by considering the paradigm: market signal, trader, response, consequence.

The analysis must begin with stage #1, the market signal. I submit that no trader will be successful who does not have access to consistently generated signals that tell him whether to buy, sell, or do nothing, as well as when to take action. Those signals may come from a sophisticated set of moving averages or from the phases of the moon. They may come from weather predictions or the *Farmer's Almanac.* It doesn't matter. What matters is that the signals are consistently and clearly generated. If this is occurring, then the analysis proceeds to stage #3, the response.

You may find it strange to jump to the response at this point in our analysis of trader behavior. Just as the technical analyst studies only the behavior of the market, however, so must we study the behavior of the trader (the response) if we are to understand the trader's performance. To illuminate this assertion, I return once again to *The Investor's Quotient.*

The significance of response is no less important to the Freudian than it is to the behaviorist. Response is, after all, another term for action, and action is the only means by which we can judge the nature of underlying processes. It follows that response, or action, is the only objective way of determining the functioning of a trader. And in order to evaluate a system, we must focus exclusively on its actions and results.

There are three reasons why the trader's action is such a crucial part of the understanding of his or her performance. First, the trader's action is the key to testing a trading system in real time. It is relatively easy to test a system on a computer; it is something else again to watch a trader work with that system. Second, action is what leads to consequences. Because of the consequence, the action always lets the trader know whether he did the right thing. Third, a study of the trader's actions allows an objective evaluation of the results.

Therefore, once it has been established that a trader is using a system that provides consistent signals, the next step is to analyze the responses to those signals. Are they consistent or inconsistent? How often is the response correct—how often is it incorrect? What are the circumstances surrounding correct and incorrect responses? Once these data are obtained, the analysis can move to stage #2, the trader, to determine whether screening is taking place and what the nature of that screening is. Then we move on to stage #4, consequences, to find out the reinforcing nature of the various consequences that occur.

## MARKET PSYCHOLOGY

Once we have a clear understanding of the behavior patterns of the individual trader, it becomes easier to understand the behavior patterns of the market. Remember the learning paradigm (Figure 9-1):

Remember that each stage of the paradigm can cause faulty reasoning to take place, resulting in behavior that is inconsistent and ultimately unprofitable. Whereas long-term market trends are closely related to the factors of supply and demand, the short and intermediate market patterns are primarily reflective of market psychology, which is simply the collective behavior of all those who are trading in the market. It is generally understood that the first buyers at the beginning of a bull move are the institutional or professional buyers, who are buying while prices are low. As prices rise, the public perceives an opportunity to profit from rising prices, and so they begin buying. Who do they buy from? In many cases, it is the professional buyers who bought at the low and who are now selling at a profit.

As the public buys into the bull market, their behavior is reinforced by accumulating profits. As more potential investors become aware of the bull market, they respond by buying in, resulting in a rapid increase in trading volume. The behavior continues to be reinforced, often handsomely. Just before the top occurs, the market typically experiences a "buying climax," which follows very bullish news, record-high trading volume, record-high prices, and very bullish public opinion. The professionals, of course, are already out of the market at this point, having recognized the clear signals of a market reversal.

The public, however, having been reinforced for jumping into the market, are oblivious to the possibility of a reversal. Their behavior has been conditioned and will continue until the reinforcement is withdrawn. Prices continue to rise at great speed until, suddenly, there seem to be no more sellers. There are only buyers, and the price race sputters and stops.

The reinforcement having now been withdrawn, a mass of buyers decides to get out of the market. Suddenly, there are more sellers than buyers, and prices begin to fall. Of course, this massive selling behavior is no more rational than the previous frenzy to buy. It is simply an attempt to cut short the losses already being experienced. The motivation for selling often seems to be purely panic at this point, as investors who see their losses mounting want to get out at any price. But, of course, now there are very few buyers, and so prices drop even lower.

At some point, of course, there are investors who believe the price has dropped low enough that it is now a bargain, and so they buy from the panicked sellers, forcing prices to stop their skid and begin rising again, thus starting the cycle over. It takes a while, however, for many of the unsophisticated traders to overcome their fear of the market—fear that has been caused by the punishment they received at the hands of the market. The classic behavioral response to punishment is avoidance, and this seems to keep the public out of the market for a while at the end of a bear slide in prices. Thus, a bull move takes much longer to form than a bear move, and it may occur again only after a period of congestion, during which prices move in a very narrow band with little trading volume.

Of course, market behavior includes many more variables than these and is more complicated than this brief scenario would lead you to believe. Nevertheless, an understanding of behavioral psychology and its application to market behavior can be very helpful as you try to make sense of the patterns that occur minute by minute, hour by hour, day by day, year after year.

Trading commodity futures is not all systems and market knowledge, supply-demand paradigms and fundamentals, economic theories, and sophisticated computer models. A study of the futures market is a study of human psychology. Therefore, self-knowledge, self-awareness, and the ability to critique your own behavior are the essential keys to success as a futures trader.

CHAPTER 10

# Participating in the Futures Industry

To many readers, the information presented thus far will have been a first glimpse into an industry that heretofore has been rather mysterious and fascinating, rather like one's first venture into a great cathedral or one of Las Vegas's most glittering casinos. To some, this brief treatise will have stripped the glitter from the fantasy and reduced it to a very pedestrian occupation requiring hard work and diligence. Others will have been inspired to pursue further studies of the various components that were discussed in the chapters of this book. All who have read to this point, however, must now realize that a simple understanding of all that has been presented here is insufficient if one wishes to be a successful futures trader.

For this book to be of real benefit, it must now present a plan of action—a strategy by which the reader can, if he or she chooses, become a part of the futures industry. To paraphrase Thomas Huxley, "The great end of (study) is not knowledge but action." Not every reader will choose to be a futures trader, and so other alternatives will also be presented.

## DEVELOPING A TRADING STRATEGY

Anyone wishing to become a futures trader will find that there is an overabundance of help available. On any weekend, somewhere in the country, some expert is presenting a seminar on a foolproof trading system. Book after book is available on technical analysis, options trading, the Elliott wave, cycles—the list goes on. Hundreds of newsletters provide advice and trading tips. Hotline phone trading advice is available from dozens of market gurus. The newcomer to futures trading finds it easy to get too much help—easy to keep taking in more information and advice.

Just as rock stars have their groupies who follow them around the country, so do commodity trading advisors have their following, many of whom never trade, but simply seek information. It is not uncommon to encounter the same individuals at seminar after seminar who, in their own words, are "collecting as much information as possible before I start trading. I want to be sure about what I'm doing before I take the risk."

For the individual who is serious about trading in the markets, however, there must be a path through this wilderness of information overload—a system for choosing the helpful from the purely extraneous. It should be obvious to anyone who has read this far that making money through futures trading is difficult to the point of being nearly impossible. On the other hand, there are traders who consistently reap tremendous profits from the futures markets. Several contemporary and legendary traders have been profiled in this book for the purpose both of inspiring the reader and of introducing the reader to real people who have been successful in the business of futures trading.

It has been mentioned already that approximately 90% of all futures traders lose money while only 10% make money. These figures seem to indicate that the cards are stacked against anyone who tries to play the game. Yet, if there are indeed futures traders who consistently make money by trading, then it would seem that success as a trader might be based on something other than simply chance.

In his book *Unlimited Power,* Tony Robbins reports on some studies that indicate that only 10% of all readers who begin reading a book read past the first chapter. This is astounding! Either 90% of all books are simply not worth reading, or 90% of all readers simply have little interest in pursuing the wisdom that is inside most books. What does this have to do with futures trading? The similarity between these two sets of seemingly unrelated statistics is piquant. In futures trading, 90% lose money. In the literary world, 90% don't pursue a book past the first chapter.

As with many statistics one encounters in life, the temptation is great to draw a correlation, even when one is not warranted by the facts. If there were any conclusions to be drawn from these two statistics, however, what might they be? Keeping in mind that there is probably no mathematical or scientific relationship between being a successful trader and reading a book through to the end, it is fun simply to speculate on this tidbit of information.

Could it be, for example, that only 10% of all the readers who first cracked the cover of this book are now reading the last chapter? If so, did that act in itself increase the probability of their success as traders? Without any empirical evidence to support a conclusion either way, the likelihood is that there is no significant relationship between finishing this book and being a successful trader. And yet, the parallel between the two statistics remains seductive.

It would be helpful, of course, to know who the 10% are who read past the first chapter and who the 10% are who are consistently successful in trading futures. To know that, however, would require an empirical study, and it is unlikely that any such study ever has been or ever will be done. And so, unfortunately, we are left to our unscientific speculations.

One possible conclusion to be drawn is that the same self-discipline and quest for knowledge that leads the 10% past the first chapter of a book also leads to a successful career in futures trading for a select few. Thus, rather than being simply a high-stakes game of chance, perhaps the futures market is really a crucible that casts aside all but the most able and the most prepared. That being so, it would behoove every would-be trader to be as prepared as possible, both emotionally and intellectually, before attempting to trade. On the other hand, being prepared also means knowing which information to ignore and which to select. With that in mind, a prospective trader needs to follow a thoughtful and well-conceived plan while developing a strategy for trading.

One such plan is outlined in the following paragraphs, which, if followed, will position a trader to take full advantage of the alternatives that the futures market has to offer. [Many of the ideas expressed in this section have already appeared in my book *Facts on Futures* (Probus Publishing, Chicago, 1987).]

*Step One: Be Honest About Factors Limiting Trading Effectiveness*

The characteristic that is most damaging to both occasional and full-time futures traders is an unrealistic view of the task and of their own strengths and limitations. The first exercise that every would-be trader must engage in is to list, in a totally honest and unbiased manner, all of the factors that might adversely affect his or her ability to trade effectively. These factors might be listed under several category headings, such as:

1. Limits on my time.

2. Financial limitations.

3. Equipment limitations.

4. Emotional limitations.

5. Other limitations.

In each of these categories, certain critical questions must be answered, such as:

1. How much time can I give the market each day (week)?

2. If I can devote time each day, is it during or after market hours?

3. Do I want to buy a computer?

4. Can I afford a computer?

5. Can I afford the exchange fees for real-time quote service?

6. How much can I comfortably allocate to a trading account?

7. Can I take the pressure of intra-day trading?

8. Can I ride large losses, or must I settle for small but more frequent losses?

9. Is my family supportive of my undertaking?

There are other questions and probably other categories that will occur to each individual who chooses to pursue this exercise. The important thing is to be honest and to let the ideas flow in a brain-storming manner: Simply write down every idea that presents itself without filtering it. Later, evaluate each thought carefully as to its validity.

### Step Two: List Goals

Again, the key is to be honest. The list may include financial, personal, social, and family goals. They may be long term or short term. Financial goals should be listed in terms of dollars or percent return on capital. After the goals have been listed, they should be reexamined in light of the previous limitations. If any goals are found to be unrealistic, they should be eliminated or modified to match the limitations. It is essential during this step that each goal be practical and workable. Any deviation from that is a setup for failure.

### Step Three: Establish a Trading Approach

At this stage, many decisions must be made. The information to assist in that decision making is available in the first 10 chapters of this book. Once the decisions have been made, however, a tremendous amount of study and preparation is necessary before effective trading can be accomplished. Some of the decisions to be made are these:

*1.* Will I try to day trade?

*2.* Will I try to scalp small profits or search for big moves?

*3.* Will I trade only futures, futures and options, or only options?

*4.* Will I try to diversify into several markets or limit my trading to one or two?

*5.* Will I approach my market analysis from a fundamental or a technical perspective?

*6.* Will I develop my own trading system or purchase one of the systems on the market?

*7.* Will I purchase a personal computer and the necessary software or do my calculations by hand?

*8.* Do I need a chart service?

Many more questions will occur to the serious trader, but each must be answered carefully and thoughtfully. Once each has a carefully considered answer, then a trading strategy will have taken shape—one that is based on a realistic appraisal of all circumstances that could either inhibit or enhance the trader's effectiveness. A trader who conscientiously completes each step of this plan is much more likely to be among the successful 10% than among the unsuccessful 90% of futures traders for two reasons. First, a trader who has thoughtfully constructed a trading strategy based on a consideration of personal limitations and the establishment of realistic goals, as well as a careful selection of components and tools, is simply better prepared than most traders. Second, and equally important, such a trader has already exhibited the discipline that is absolutely necessary if a trader is to be consistently successful. Without discipline, the best plan and strategy will ultimately fail. It is very likely that most of the failures of the 90% can be laid at the feet of either poor preparation or poor discipline, or both, because they seem to go hand in hand.

## CHOOSING A TRADING SYSTEM

Once an individual has conscientiously completed each step of the foregoing exercise and still honestly feels that he or she wishes to become a trader, it is time to choose a trading system. There are on the market numerous canned computerized systems that make fantastic claims of profitability. Such claims, of course, must be analyzed carefully. Does the hypothetical performance cover a sufficient period of time? Many trading systems will work quite well under limited market conditions but fall apart in the long haul as conditions change. Has the system been tested in real time and for a sufficient period of time? Real-time trading, with its accompanying imperfections, such as poor fills, bad timing, and unexpected surprises, is totally different from hypothetical trading, which uses historical information that is immune to the quirks and imperfections of the fast-paced market in real time.

In hypothetical trading, there is always only one alternative available for the market to behave: the way it did behave. In real-time trading, there are infinite alternatives available for market behavior, only a few of which will return a profit to the individual trader. Therefore, how has this system performed in real time—paying commissions, suffering slippage, and under the imperfect implementation of a real human trader?

Has the system been molded to historical price data and market conditions? In analyzing historical data and developing specific responses to that data, a computer will produce a system that is optimal for that data and under those specific conditions. Such a system, however, often lacks the flexibility to adapt to changing real-time conditions. Thus, a system with a poor hypothetical performance may do better in real-time trading, over time, than a system with fantastic hypothetical results.

In choosing a trading system, be aware that a system does not have to be highly sophisticated, computerized, or complicated. Some of the best trading systems require only a few simple hand computations to generate reasonably accurate buy or sell signals. To be acceptable, however, any trading system must minimally do the following:

*1.* Provide accurate entry and exit signals. The accuracy rate should be in excess of 65% to 75%.

*2.* Provide a specific method of entry and exit after generating the signals.

*3.* Establish a specific objective or reversal point.

*4.* Establish money management conditions, i.e., stop-loss points, amount to risk, etc.

*5.* Avoid periods of severe drawdown.

This last point is very important. Many systems that produce fantastic hypothetical trading records over many years will, upon closer examination, generate periods of severe drawdowns. Most traders cannot emotionally or financially withstand such extended periods of loss. Therefore, such a system, no matter how potentially profitable, may be unrealistic for most traders.

## CREATING YOUR OWN SYSTEM

In recent years, even more sophisticated software has been developed that allows a trader to create a personal computerized trading system by testing infinite models on historical data. A trader who really wants to get into the business can use such software to optimize technical and mechanical systems to each market and to certain identifiable aspects of individual markets. (If a trader wishes to investigate such systems, I would refer him or her to one of the originators of such software systems, Lou Mendelsohn and Associates, 50 Meadow Lane, Zephyr Hills, Florida 34249.) As with all trading systems and approaches, however, this path is not fool-proof and is fraught with liabilities and potential snafus. There are, nevertheless, traders who have diligently approached the task and have been rewarded with systems that work reasonably well and return reasonable profits.

## ALTERNATIVES TO BEING AN ACTIVE TRADER

Most individuals approaching the futures market will find that the commitment of time and energy necessary to learn about the markets and to maintain a disciplined trading program is simply too great. Unfortunately, many will continue to trade on their own—dabbling—as some call it, and by so doing they will place themselves firmly among the 90% of losers, except, of course, for the occasional big winner that they can brag about at cocktail parties and around the office water cooler.

Others, realizing that such a course of action is much too risky, and not being of a mind to give away their money but still being interested in participating in the futures markets, will look for alternatives to trading on their own. Among the alternatives available to them are commodity funds, managed accounts, directed hot lines and broker discretionary trading. Each has its advantages and disadvantages, but the disciplined individual who approaches such alternatives carefully and with the same degree of scrutiny used earlier in developing a trading strategy will find each of these alternatives to be viable and potentially profitable.

### Commodity Funds

A recent addition to the world of futures trading is the *commodity fund,* or *limited partnership.* Based on the concept of a stock mutual fund, investors buy units of a commodity fund, which are then pooled, and the money is traded by a professional trading advisor or, in some cases, a group of advisors. Most funds are closed end—that is, once the initial offering is sold out, no more units are offered publicly. The minimum investment is usually $5,000, or five $1,000 units. Most funds also qualify for Individual Retirement Account (IRA) deposits.

There are those who say that commodity funds mark the coming of age of the futures industry—that funds have opened futures trading to many who would not have considered investing in futures previously. Certainly, the funds are a popular investment vehicle. From only a few funds in 1979, by 1988 there were over 120 funds being traded, with more being added each month.

The popularity of futures funds is derived from four factors:

*1.* Low initial investment. Many people are willing to risk $5,000 in a fund who are not willing to risk $20,000 to $30,000 in a professionally managed account or in their own trading account.

*2.* Reasonable limited risk. Most funds have a clause in the prospectus that stipulates the fund will cease trading and return all assets if the total equity in the fund sinks to 50% of its original size. This means there is a reasonable likelihood that each investor will lose no more than half of his or her original investment. When compared to the unlimited risk of futures trading, where the original investment can be lost as well as additional money required to meet a margin call, this characteristic of a fund is very attractive.

*3.* Professional management. The trading advisors to a fund are usually veteran traders with a proven track record. An investor in a futures fund can be reasonably certain that the person or persons with whom his or her money is entrusted is a competent trader with proven expertise. On another level, the general partners of the fund are usually knowledgeable about futures trading and money management and will carefully monitor the progress of the trading that goes on in the fund account.

*4.* Diversification. Because a futures fund pools several million dollars in a trading account, the account can be traded on several markets by several advisors, providing the diversification that would be impossible to obtain if the $5,000 investment were traded in a personal account.

As attractive as futures funds seem, however, there are some disadvantages and some pitfalls that the investor must be wary of. One disadvantage is that the money is tied up in a fund for a minimum time period—often six months from the time of investment. Thereafter, the money can be taken out only when and if the units can be resold. Thus, a futures fund is not a liquid investment vehicle. Second, although several of the best performing futures funds do as well as or better than the best mutual funds, it is not uncommon for a futures fund to lose money rather than to make money. Therefore, a fund must be chosen very carefully, with a sharp eye toward the track record of the advisors. Third, funds can be expensive. Many funds charge management fees up front, thereby reducing the amount of the initial investment. Others charge no management fees but do charge advisory incentive fees as a percentage of profits. Moreover, the amount of commissions charged for each trade varies considerably among funds.

A careful trader who is considering putting money in a futures fund should therefore approach the task very cautiously. If the fund has been trading for several months, its performance can be tracked through *Futures Magazine* or *Managed Account Reports,* both of which report on the actual profits or losses of over 120 futures funds. If the fund is new, the track records of each of the advisors should be checked carefully.

### Managed Accounts

Another popular vehicle for traders who lack the time or expertise to trade their own accounts is a professionally *managed account.* With this kind of program, the trader establishes a personal trading account with a broker but signs a limited power of attorney that transfers discretionary trading authority to a selected futures trader who usually is a registered Commodity Trading Advisor (CTA). All of the trading decisions are made by the CTA, but daily trade confirmations, monthly purchases, and sale summaries are sent to the person in whose name the account was opened.

One advantage of an individual managed account is the liquidity of the investment. The account holder can take money out, add money, request that trading cease, or close the account at any time, with proper notice being given. Another advantage is that the managed account can be monitored closely, allowing the account holder to close the account if he or she does not like the way the CTA is managing it.

Managed accounts do have disadvantages and, as with futures funds, must be approached very cautiously. First, the management fees can be excessive. Some CTAs charge only an incentive fee as a percentage of the profits. This can range from 50% down to 10%. Others charge a management fee, which is often subtracted from the account each month, whether a profit is made or not. Second, brokerage commissions vary significantly, from the equivalent of discount commissions to full-service commissions. If a CTA trades frequently, the cost of commissions can add up to a significant drain on the account. Third, the CTA who trades the account may have a trading style that conflicts with the personal nature of the account holder. For example, the CTA may be a very cautious trader, careful to avoid large losses while being content to take small profits on a high frequency of good trades. The account holder, meanwhile, would like to see his or her account traded in a very aggressive manner, willing to sit through large drawdowns in the interest of catching highly profitable trades. Such a match, obviously, will lead to problems between the CTA and the account holder.

A fourth disadvantage with a managed account is that CTAs often require rather large initial investments. Many expect at least $25,000 while some require $50,000 to open an account. A final danger is that the account holder is subject to unlimited risk. A major drawdown can deplete the account and leave the account holder liable for additional losses.

To avoid some of the potential pitfalls of a professionally managed account, the prior performance of a CTA should be evaluated very carefully. Each CTA must provide a disclosure document to any person expressing an interest in a managed account. This document will describe the trading strategy to be followed, the markets that will be traded, the minimum investment required, and the fees to be charged.

Additionally, the disclosure will detail the CTA's track record for at least the past three years and sometimes longer. This track record must be evaluated carefully, as it will reveal a great deal about the trading style of the CTA. The actual percentage of profits can be misleading, as there are two different NFA-approved formulas for constructing a track record, each of which handles equity additions and withdrawals differently, resulting in radically different percentages of gain or loss figures. Still, the figures should indicate consistent profitability over a reasonable time span. The size of the gains that are acceptable is subject to the judgment of the prospective client. Some individuals may be content with relatively low returns in exchange for small losses, whereas others may want to see gains of at least 100% per year to justify the risk of futures trading.

Just as important as the percentage of gain, then, is the percentage of loss. How many months of gain are there in relation to the months showing a loss? What is the largest loss in a month or a quarter? Is this a loss that would be tolerable? Is the total profitability for the year based on only one or two very profitable months? Or were there consistent profits month after month? In 1987, for example, many CTAs showed extremely profitable years because they happened to be on the short side of the S&P 500 Index in October during the crash. This return was not consistent with their usual performance and thus should be discounted.

In evaluating a CTA, therefore, one must look at the trading consistency, the profitability over a reasonable span of time, and the size of drawdowns versus the amount of profits. The resulting profile should be consistent with the prospective client's own goals and emotional profile. If the two don't match, then another CTA should be chosen.

### Directed Hot Lines

A relatively new service offered by some brokers is the *directed hot line.* With this service, a trader chooses a hot-line advisory service he or she likes and then gives the broker the authority to call the hot line and place the trades exactly as recommended. This service works very much like a managed account, but rather than paying a management fee, the client pays a fee for the hot-line service.

Many traders who don't have the time to do the necessary market research but still want to be actively involved in trading find that an advisory service, particularly one with a daily hot-line recommendation, is an ideal solution. With this kind of service, the trader need only call the hot-line number each day to find out which trades are being recommended, then call his or her broker to place the trade. The advantage of this kind of service is that the trader has ultimate control over his or her account and can choose whether to make a trade and when to cease trading or resume trading. The trader can also select a discount broker, thus saving commission costs. The disadvantage is that many such services can be very expensive, and it may be difficult to find an advisory service that is compatible with the trader's own goals and trading style.

To choose the correct advisory service, a trader must be very careful to examine thoroughly the services being offered. Many hot lines make fantastic claims that, upon closer examination, tend to evaporate. Of critical concern is how specific the recommendations are. Does the hot line recommend what to buy, when to buy, and a price to buy at? Or is the recommendation simply a vague statement open to interpretation and leaving all the decision making to the trader? It's easy to claim a fantastic performance record when the performance is based on 20/20 hindsight.

A second concern when choosing a hot-line advisory is whether the timing of the recommendations permits real-time implementation. An advisory service is no good if the trades are signaled too late to implement them.

A third concern is whether the trader has the time and equipment to follow the recommendations. Some hot lines require order entry and update during the day. Others require real-time price information. Both situations may be unrealistic for a trader who works a very busy daytime job.

Fourth, a good advisory service should also provide specific price or time objectives, stop-loss points, and specific follow-up procedures that will leave a trader with alternatives regardless of market conditions. Some services, unfortunately, are excellent at getting a trader into the market but vague and nonspecific about getting him or her out.

When checking the performance record of a hot line, it is important to note certain items. First, is the claimed performance based on unrealistic and hypothetical circumstances? Some hot lines, for instance, have been known, in their hypothetical trading, to take extremely large positions, to scale into the market holding losing positions, to purchase or sell extremely large numbers of contracts, or to add more margin to the hypothetical account so as to withstand most losing positions. Such a trading strategy is unrealistic for most small traders, who should not hold more than five to 10 positions at any one time.

Second, a trader must look closely at the largest single loss, the largest single profit, the average loss, the average profit, and the win-lose percentage ratio to determine whether the hot line matches his or her preferred style. Some services make most of their profits on a few big trades while suffering a large number of small losses. Others will make many small gains and few small losses. Still others will encounter a few large gains and a few large drawdowns.

Third, if the performance record is hypothetical, it is important that the amount deducted for commissions and bad fills be realistic. Generally, this should be in the neighborhood of $100 per trade.

Fourth, is the track record built on trading markets that are too volatile and risky for a small trader?

Fifth, does the hypothetical performance require a realistic level of margin? If a trader plans to trade an account of $20,000, the hot line cannot recommend trades that would exceed that margin without adversely affecting the performance of the trader's account.

As a final comment, the trader wishing to use the services of a carefully chosen hot line must be prepared to trade his or her account consistent with the recommendations. The published performance record of the hot line is based on making all the trades. A trader who picks and chooses the trades will of necessity perform differently than the hot-line performance. Because such behavior will be based on little more than intuition or feeling, it will more than likely place the trader among the 90% of losers but will allow for a great deal of cocktail party bragging when the occasional recommended trade goes particularly sour and the trader (wisely, of course) stayed out.

### Broker-Assisted and Broker Discretionary Trading

Probably the most common way many small traders experience the market is by trading a small account on the recommendation of a broker. Occasionally, a trader will give discretionary authority to a broker to trade the account without seeking approval on every trade. If a trader chooses this avenue, the same rules apply for checking the track record, since there will likely be no published figures to pursue; however, the trader must have confidence in the integrity of the broker. With *broker-assisted* and *broker discretionary trading,* there is also the potential conflict of interest to be concerned with—the broker's reward comes from the number of trades made, not the quality of the individual trades.

# CHAPTER 11

# Making the Futures Market Work For You

What you have read in this book is intended to serve as a very basic introduction to the futures markets and futures trading. I have attempted to achieve the following goals in the preceding chapters:

*1.* to introduce the basic concepts underlying futures trading and the futures markets;

*2.* to explain the economic functions of futures trading;

*3.* to explain the role of the speculators, hedgers, commercial interests, and brokers in the futures markets;

*4.* to provide a general understanding of fundamental and technical analysis and to give examples of each; and

*5.* to highlight the various aspects of the futures industry as well as different opportunities available to you whether as an independent trader, broker, or market analyst.

In order to achieve a thorough understanding of this challenging but rewarding field, I suggest you consider the following steps:

*1. Learn more.* Throughout this book I have stressed the value and, indeed, the necessity of education. If you plan to seriously pursue either a job in the area of futures trading or if you plan to trade for your own account, you must learn as much as you can. There are literally hundreds of books for beginners and advanced students and many classroom courses you can take.

*2. Get your "feet wet."* Once you've taken the time to learn more from books and/or coursework, get involved in futures trading. Open a small account and trade for yourself or work with a broker. Don't risk a great deal, particularly if you can't afford it. Consider the money you put into your account as part of your tuition. If you lose it, you've helped further your education; if you win, you've learned something as well as having something to show for it other than just learning itself.

*3. Ask questions.* Be sure to ask questions. If you know other traders, use them as resources to learn more. If you open a trading account, ask your broker questions. You'll learn more by asking questions than you will from any book. Best of all, the answers usually won't cost you anything!

4. *Visit a broker's office.* You can learn a great deal by watching brokers do their work. If you have the opportunity to watch your broker work, do so. You'll get to see exactly how orders are entered, time stamped, and reported back to the broker and customers. This will further your understanding of the different types of orders, when they are used, and how to use them.

5. *Visit one of the futures exchanges.* Every futures exchange provides public tours. Take some time and visit the exchanges. The first-hand experience of witnessing the markets in real-time operation will add to your appreciation of: how the futures markets work; the role of traders, runners, and exchange officials; computerized price reporting; government regulation; and more. Even after all of my years as a futures trader, I still enjoy an occasional visit to the exchange. If you know someone who can get you onto the trading floor, this may be an even more exciting educational thing to do.

6. *Consider a job as a "runner."* Many successful traders and brokers have started as runners on the trading floor of one or more futures exchanges. The experience has been valuable in spite of the very poor salary usually earned by runners. If you have the opportunity to get such a job, you'll learn more in two weeks on the floor than you can in several years of academic studies. This is perhaps the single best way to get an education in the futures industry. If you have the financial means to support yourself while you take a runner's job, then by all means do so!

7. *Subscribe to some newsletters or send for free samples.* See what some of the trading advisors and money managers have to say. More important, see how they say it—learn market vocabulary; become familiar with the issues; and gain an understanding of risks, rewards, methods of analysis, strategies, and more. There are literally hundreds of services, most of them providing you with a wealth of information and samples at no cost whatsoever.

*8. Read some of the trade publications.* While such regular reading as the *Wall Street Journal* will keep you informed on current events, it is helpful to regularly read such trade publications as *Futures Magazine*. While it may not be a good idea to take anything you read in these publications too seriously, it is a good idea to keep informed on industry trends and events.

*9. Do your own research.* If you have some market ideas of your own, don't be afraid to test them. Home computer systems, historical futures data, and analytical software are so reasonably priced nowadays that systems testing is not as expensive a proposition as it was in the past. If you have ideas about trading systems that merit further investigation and development and if you have the funds to pursue this direction, then I encourage you to do so.

These are just a few suggestions that may help you to develop your skills or find employment in the futures industry. How you use this information and what you eventually decide to do is, of course, a matter of individual preference. I do, however, encourage you to consider being involved in futures trading one way or another

In closing, I feel that I must also address an issue which has become prominent in the late 1980s. As many of you know, there have been investigations, allegations, and charges of wrong-doing by some floor traders in the Chicago markets. This has, of course, given the futures market what I feel is undeservedly negative publicity. For the most part I have found that the futures industry has done an excellent job policing itself. The Commodity Futures Trading Commission and the National Futures Association have, through the years, done a good job regulating futures trading. Certainly there is always the possibility that unethical and illegal practices will occur. This is true in any industry. As you know, even the stock market and major stock brokerage firms have not been immune to such shortcomings. Yet we must all remember that it is up to the individual to assume responsibility for his or her own actions. It is up to the consumer to be careful and mindful of who he or she is dealing with. The rules and regulations are there to protect both the public and the professionals. We must follow them accordingly. If, however, we feel that the rules are bad, or that they infringe on more essential rights, then we must also act to change them. Our system of government and our judicial system provide the appropriate channels for doing so. I do not feel that any individual should be dissuaded from becoming involved in futures trading due to concerns about the ethics of this industry. Ultimately the greater good will overcome the minor amount of evil as well as the negative publicity.

# References and Reading List

Allen, R. C. *How to Use the Four-Day, Nine-Day, and 19-Day Moving Average to Earn Larger Profits from Commodities.* Chicago: Best Books, 1974.

Angrist, Stanley W. *Sensible Speculating in Commodities.* N.Y.: Simon & Schuster, 1972.

Appleman, Mark J. *The Winning Habit: How Your Personality Makes You a Winner or Loser in the Stock Market.* N.Y.: McCall, 1970.

Arthur, Henry B. *Commodity Futures as a Business Management Tool.* Cambridge, Mass.: Harvard University Press, 1971.

Babcock, Bruce Jr. *The Dow Jones-Irwin Guide to Trading Systems.* Homewood, Ill.: Richard D. Irwin Inc., 1989.

Barnes, Robert M. *Taming the Pits: A Technical Approach to Commodity Trading.* N.Y.: John Wiley & Sons, 1979.

Baruch, Bernard. *My Own Story.* N.Y.: Holt, 1957.

Bernstein, Jacob. *The Investor's Quotient.* N.Y.: John Wiley & Sons, 1981.

Bernstein, Jacob. *The Handbook of Commodity Cycles: A Window on Time.* N.Y.: John Wiley & Sons, 1982.

Bernstein, Jacob. *How to Profit in Precious Metals.* N.Y.: John Wiley & Sons, 1985.

Bernstein, Jacob. *Beyond the Investor's Quotient.* N.Y.: John Wiley & Sons, 1986.

Bernstein, Jacob. *Facts on Futures.* Chicago: Probus Publishing, 1987.

Bernstein, Jacob. *Short Term Trading in Futures.* Chicago: Probus Publishing, 1987.

Bernstein, Jacob. *Seasonal Cash Chart Study.* Winnetka, Ill.: MBH Commodity, 1988.

Bernstein, Jacob. *Cyclic Analysis in Futures Trading.* N.Y.: John Wiley & Sons, 1988.

Bernstein, Jacob. *MBH Seasonal Futures Charts a Study of Weekly Seasonal Tendencies in the Commodity Futures Markets.* Winnetka, Ill.: MBH Commodity, 1988.

Bernstein, Jacob. *The Analysis and Forecasting of Long-Term Trends in the Cash and Futures Markets.* Chicago: Probus Publishing, 1989.

Blumenthal, Earl. *Chart for Profit: Point & Figure Trading.* Larchmont, N.Y.: Investors Intelligence, 1975.

Bolton, A. Hamilton. *The Elliott Wave Principle: A Critical Appraisal.* Hamilton, Bermuda: Monetary Research, 1960.

Clasing, H. *The Dow Jones-Irwin Guide to Put and Call Options.* Homewood, Ill.: Dow Jones-Irwin, 1978.

*Contrary Opinion.* Hadady Corporation, 1111 S. Arroyo Parkway, Suite 410, Pasadena, Calif. 91109–0490, 1983.

*Cycles.* Foundation for the Study of Cycles, 3333 Michelson Drive, Irvine, Calif. 92715.

Dewey, Edward R. *Cycles, Selected Writings.* Pittsburgh: Foundation for the Study of Cycles, 1970.

Dewey, Edward R. *Cycles, the Mysterious Forces that Trigger Events.* N.Y.: Hawthorne Books, 1971.

*The Dow Jones Commodities Handbook: A Guide to Major Futures Markets.* Princeton, N.J.: Dow Jones Books, 1983.

Dunn, D. and E. Hargitt. *Point and Figure Commodity Trading: A Computer Evaluation.* West Lafayette, Ind.: Dunn and Hargitt, 1971.

*Futures Magazine.* 219 Parkade, Cedar Falls, Iowa 50613.

Gann, William D. *Forty-Five Years in Wall Street.* Pomeroy, Wash.: Lambert-Gann, 1949.

Gann, William D. *How to Make Profits in Commodities.* Rev. ed. Pomeroy, Wash.: Lambert-Gann, 1951.

Gann, William D. *The Basis of My Forecasting Method for Grain.* Pomeroy, Wash.: Lambert-Gann, 1970 (originally 1935).

Gann, William D. *Forecasting Grains by Time Cycles.* Pomeroy, Wash.: Lambert-Gann, 1976.

Gann, William D. *Forecasting Rules for Cotton.* Pomeroy, Wash.: Lambert-Gann, 1976.

Gann, William D. *Forecasting Rules for Gain-Geometric Angles.* Pomeroy, Wash.: Lambert-Gann, 1976.

Gold, Gerald. *Modern Commodity Futures Trading.* 7th ed. N.Y.: Commodity Research Bureau, 1975.

Goss, B. A. and B. S. Yamey. *The Economics of Futures Trading.* N.Y.: John Wiley & Sons, 1976.

Hieronymus, Thomas. *Economics of Futures Trading for Commercial and Personal Profit.* N.Y.: Commodity Research Bureau, 1977.

Hieronymus, Thomas A. *Economics of Futures Trading for Commercial and Personal Profit.* 2nd ed. N.Y.: Commodity Research Bureau, 1977.

Hill, John R. *Scientific Interpretation of Bar Charts.* Hendersonville, N.C.: Commodity Research Institute, 1979.

Hill, John R. *Stock and Commodity Market Trend Trading by Advanced Technical Analysis.* Hendersonville, N.C.: Commodity Research Institute, 1977.

Hoppe, Donald J. *The Kondratieff Wave Analyst.* Box 977, Crystal Lake, Ill. 60014.

Huff, Charles. *Commodity Speculation for Beginners: A Guide to the Futures Markets.* N.Y.: Macmillan, 1980.

Hurst, J. M. *The Profit Magic of Stock Transaction Timing.* Englewood Cliffs, N.J.: Prentice-Hall, 1970.

*Intermarket Magazine.* 141 W. Jackson, Chicago, Ill. 60604.

Jiler, Harry, ed. *Forecasting Commodity Prices: How the Experts Analyze the Market.* N.Y.: Commodity Research Bureau, 1975.

Kaufman, Perry J. *Commodity Trading Systems and Methods.* N.Y.: John Wiley & Sons, 1978.

Kaufman, Perry J. *Technical Analysis in Commodities.* N.Y.: John Wiley & Sons, 1980.

Keltner, C. W. *How to Make Money in Commodities.* Kansas City, Mo.: Keltner Statistical Service, 1960.

Kindleberger, Charles P. *Manias, Panics and Crashes: A History of Financial Crisis.* N.Y.: Basic Books, 1978.

Kroll, Stanley and Irwin Shisko. *The Commodity Futures Market Guide.* N.Y.: Harper & Row, 1973.

Lefevre, Edwin. *Reminiscences of a Stock Operator.* N.Y.: American Research Council, 1923. Reprint ed., Burlington, Vt.: Books of Wall Street, 1980.

Leslie, Conrad. *Conrad Leslie's Guide for Successful Speculating.* Chicago: Dartnell Press, 1970.

McMillan, L. *Options as a Strategic Investment.* N.Y.: New York Institute of Finance, 1980.

Oster, Merrill J. *Commodity Futures for Profit . . . A Farmer's Guide to Hedging.* Cedar Falls, Iowa: Investor Publications, 1979.

Oster, Merrill J. *Professional Hedging Handbook: A Guide to Hedging Crops and Livestock.* Cedar Falls, Iowa: Investor Publications, 1979.

Powers, Mark J. *Getting Started in Commodity Futures Trading.* 2nd ed. Cedar Falls, Iowa: Investor Publications, 1977.

Reinach, Anthony M. *The Fastest Game in Town: Trading Commodity Futures.* N.Y.: Commodity Research Bureau, 1973.

Sharpe, William F. *Investments.* Englewood Cliffs, N.J.: Prentice-Hall, 1978.

Smith, A. *The Money Game.* New York: Random House, 1967.

Teweles, Richard J., Charles V. Harlow, and Herbert L. Stone. *The Commodity Futures Game—Who Wins? Who Loses? Why?* 2nd ed. N.Y.: McGraw-Hill, 1974.

Williams, Larry R. and Michelle Noseworthy. *Sure Thing Commodity Trading, How Seasonal Factors Influence Commodity Prices.* Brightwaters, N.Y.: Windsor, 1977.

# Glossary

*Arbing.* See Arbitrage.

*Arbitrage.* The simultaneous purchase of one commodity against the sale of another in order to profit from distortions from usual price relationships. Variations include simultaneous purchase and sale of different delivery months of the same commodity, of the same commodity and delivery month on two different exchanges, and the purchase of one commodity against the sale of another commodity.

See also *Spread.*

*Arbitraging.* See Arbitrage.

*Back Month.* A calendar month that is active and more than 90 days from the current trading month.

*Example:*

| | | | | | |
|---|---|---|---|---|---|
| Active Months | Mar | May | Jun | Jul | Dec |
| Current Month | Mar | | | | |
| Back Months | | | | Jul | Dec |

Sometimes this term is used to signify a month in which futures trading is taking place with a maturity other than current spot.

*Example:*

| | | | | | |
|---|---|---|---|---|---|
| Active Months | Mar | May | Jun | Jul | Dec |
| Current Month | Mar | | | | |
| Back Months | | May | Jun | Jul | Dec |

*Bar Chart.* A graph of horizontal bars or vertical columns comparing characteristics of two or more items or showing differing proportions of those items. Bar charts are used in technical analysis to track price ranges and movements.

*Basis.* The difference between a cash price at a specific location and the price of a particular futures contract.

*Bottom.* Lowest price reached during a market cycle.

*Call Option.* An exchange-traded option contract that gives the purchaser the right, but not the obligation, to enter into an underlying futures contract to buy a commodity at a stated strike price any time prior to the option's expiration date. The grantor of the call has the obligation, upon exercise, to deliver the long futures.

*Example: The buyer (traded)*

| Option | Strike Price | Expire Date | Trade Price |
|---|---|---|---|
| October 12: | | | |
| Long 1 Mar Sugar #11 | @ 1200 | March 9 | 1.20 |

During the dates of October 12 and March 9 of the next year, the March futures market trades at 1400.

The buyer exercises the right to be long (the futures) at 1200 (option strike price):

| | | | | |
|---|---|---|---|---|
| *Futures* Long 1 | Mar Sugar #11 | @ 1200 | | |
| *Market* | Mar Sugar #11 | @ 1400 | | |
| (transaction) | Points | + | 200 | gain |
| Buyer paid option | Points | − | 120 | |
| premium: | Net Points | | 80 | gain |

(Less commission and fees upon ultimate sale of the futures.)

*Carrying Charges.* Those costs incurred in warehousing the physical commodity, generally including interest, insurance, and storage.

*Cash Settlement.* A finalizing mechanism in which a contract is satisfied with a cash value calculation. Cash may be given in lieu of the actual commodity, or it may be required in addition to physical delivery of a commodity (for example, when commodity quality necessitates a premium or a discount). In finalizing a financial product, such as an index or foreign-exchange product, cash settlement is necessary because the contract represents a value rather than a physical product.

*Clearinghouse.* An agency connected with a commodity exchange through which all futures contracts are reconciled, settled, guaranteed, and later either offset or fulfilled through delivery of the commodity and through which financial settlement is made. It may be a fully chartered separate corporation rather than a division of the exchange itself.

*Commodity Fund.* Investment pool, observed as a limited partnership, formed to speculate in commodity futures and options. Each participant (investor) will have his or her original investment increased (reduced) by his or her proportional share of income and trading profits (expenses and trading losses).

*Crush Spread ("Crushers").* This position entails long soybean futures contracts and short soybean oil and soybean meal futures contracts in fixed proportions. It is called a crush spread because this replicates the positions taken by soybean processors when hedging the later purchase of inputs and sale of products.

*Cyclic Analysis.* Analysis that uses various seasonal factors as a basis to determine trends and prices.

*Delta.* A percentage value of the amount that an option premium can be expected to change for a given unit change in the underlying futures contract.

The factor takes into consideration the time remaining to an option's expiration, the volatility of the underlying futures contract, and the price relationship.

> *Example:* Formula to calculate the delta factor for S & P 500 options:

Factors are available from all the clearinghouses offering option trading. They change on a daily basis.

*Demand.* The quantities of a commodity that potential buyers would want to purchase at different prices given current conditions (e.g., prices of related goods, expectations, tastes, etc.). The quantity of commodity demanded is inversely related to price.

*Discretionary Trading.* Customer accounts where specified employees of a brokerage firm may execute trades without explicit authorization of every individual transaction.

*Dollar Value (or Cash Value).* The monetary value of the full amount of a commodity or financial instrument represented by a futures contract. This is the price per unit times the number of units.

> *Examples:* Grain futures—$5.00/bu × 5,000 bu = $25,000 or T-Bond or T-Note future—87 − 16/32 × $100,000 = $87,500.

*Elasticity of Demand (Supply).* The percentage change in quantities demanded (supplied) for a given percentage change in price. Inelastic demand (supply) would indicate relatively small changes in quantities compared to the price change. Elastic demand (supply) would indicate relatively large changes in quantities compared to the price change.

*Elliott Wave.* Theory of cyclical movements of prices. Follows certain indicators that predict and confirm price movements.

*Exercise Price.* The predetermined price level(s) at which an underlying futures contract or actual commodity may be established upon exercise of the option. For futures options, the exchange sets a price in line with the previous day's settlement price for the underlying futures. From that price, exercise prices at exchange-determined intervals above and below are established. Options may be traded at these exercise prices. Each successive day, new prices may be established in addition to those currently trading and/ or available for trading if the futures market fluctuations warrant it.

*Expiration Date.* The last day that an option may be exercised into the underlying futures/actual commodity contract. If not exercised or assigned, the option ceases to exist.

*Fibonacci Ratios.* Ratios of cyclical market movements to one another that are used to establish price objectives concerning the likely movements in the next cycle.

*Fill-or-Kill Order.* An order that must be offered or bid immediately at a given price and canceled if not executed. The standard abbreviation is *FOK.* Also known as *Immediate Order, FOK.*

> *Example:*
>
> Buy 1 Dec COMEX Gold @ 400.00 Fill or Kill
>
> may also be written as
>
> B 1 Z COMEX GLD @ 400.00 FOK

*Floor Manager.* A brokerage firm employee responsible for overseeing and coordinating the activities of all the trading floor personnel of the firm: runners, phone clerks, traders, and assistants.

*Floor Supervisor.* See Floor Manager.

*Foreign Currency Future.* A contract requiring the later purchase and sale of a designated amount of money issued by a foreign bank. (As a March Swiss franc contract would call for the delivery of 125,000 francs during a specified period in March.)

*Full Carrying Charge Market.* A situation in the futures market when the price difference between delivery months reflects the full costs of interest, insurance, and storage.

*Futures Contract.* An agreement to later buy or sell a commodity of a standardized amount and standardized minimum quality grade, during a specific month, under terms and conditions established by the federally designated contract market upon which trading is conducted, at a price established in the trading pit.

*Futures Option.* An option contract, exercise of which results in the holder and writer of the option exchanging futures positions.

*Good-Till-Canceled Order.* An order to buy or sell at a fixed price that remains open until executed or canceled by the customer.

---

*Example:*

Buy 1 Dec COMEX Gold @ 420.00 Good-Till-Canceled

---

may also be written as

---

B 1 Z COMEX GLD @ 420.00 GTC

---

*Note:* Provision may be made to cancel automatically on a given day.

*Example:* An order entered on March 10

---

Buy 1 Dec COMEX Gold @ 420.00 Good-Till Mar 15

---

*Hedging.* The initiation of a position in a futures market that is intended as a temporary substitute for the sale or purchase of the actual commodity. The sale of futures contracts in anticipation of future sales of cash commodities as a protection against possible price declines, or the purchase of futures contracts in anticipation of future purchases of cash commodities as a protection against the possibility of increasing costs.

*Initial Margin.* Cash or securities required as a good-faith deposit to establish a specific, new position in the futures or option market. An initial margin amount is set by the respective exchange.

Note: Initial margin is not a partial payment of the purchase.

*Inter-commodity Spread.* The purchase and sale of two different, but related, commodities with the same delivery month and trading on the same exchange.

*Inter-market Spread.* The purchase and sale of the same commodity on two different exchanges.

*Example:*

---

*Chicago Board of Trade (CBT)*

---

Long 5 Mar Silver (1,0000 oz. each)

---

*New York Commodity Exchange (COMEX)*

---

Short 1 Mar Silver (5,000 oz.)

---

*Interest Rate Future.* A contract reflecting the value (and usually the later purchase or sale) of debt instruments (as T-Bond, T-Bill, Eurodollar Deposit, or Municipal Bond Futures).

*Intra-market Spread.* The purchase of a commodity and sale of the same commodity of a different contract month or of a different commodity of the same or a different month, both contracts of which are trading on the same exchange.

*Example:*

---

*Chicago Board of Trade*

---

Long 5M May Wheat
Short 5M July Wheat

---

*Limit Order.* An order with some restriction(s), such as price, time, or both, on execution. Restrictions are set by the client.

*Example:* Time limit—

---

Buy 1 Apr Gold @ 400.00 Opening Only

---

may also be written as

---

B 1 J GLD @ 400.00 Opening Only

---

*Example:* Price limit—

---

Buy 1 Apr Gold @ 390.00

---

may also be written as

---

B 1 J GLD @ 390.00

---

*Limited Partnership.* Business organization wiith full flow-through of the consequence to the partners. Limited partners' liabilities are limited to their investment plus any debt they have agreed to be charged for. Limited partnerships must have one or more general partners whose liability is unlimited.

*Liquidity.* Refers to the least cost at which one can enter and then close out a position.

*Local (Broker).* A floor broker who may trade for customers but primarily for his or her own account, continuously buying and selling for quick profits.

*Maintenance Margin.* The monetary value to which the original margin requirement may depreciate and still be considered a satisfactory margin to carry the established position. A minimum is specified by the governing exchange, but it may be the policy of an individual firm to set a minimum higher than the governing exchange's. *Also known as:* Variation Allowance.

*Example:*

| | |
|---|---|
| *Initial Requirement 1 Contract* | *$4,000.00* |
| *Allowable Market Fluctuation (negative)* | *−1,000.00* |
| *Maintenance Level for the Contract* | *$3,000.00* |

*Note:* The rule of thumb is maintenance at 75% of the original requirement.

*Managed Accounts.* Customer accounts where all trades are determined by a trading advisor or fund manager.

*Market Analyst.* An individual that follows all important factors potentially affecting the price of the commodity or financial instrument in question. Market analysts typically distribute analyses of past market movement and forecasts of futures developments.

*Market Order.*  An order to buy or sell a specified number of contracts for a specified commodity month at the best price available at the time the order reaches the trading ring. *Also known as:* Market order.

| *Example:* |
| --- |
| Buy 5M May Wheat Market |
| may also be written as |
| B 5M K WHT MKT |

As long as the execution price represents the best offering at the time of execution and the price received was traded approximately at the time the order entered the trading ring, any price is acceptable.

*Market-if-Touched Order.* A contingency order given with a limited price instruction, that when the market reaches the required price level, it becomes a market order to trade at the next best trading price. This term is also known by the standard abbreviation *MIT.*

| *Example:* |
| --- |
| Buy 1 Dec Gold @ 320.00 Market if Touched |
| may also be written as |
| b 1 Z GLD @ 320.00 MIT |

This buy order is placed below the marker and is not to be executed unless and until the market reaches 320.00. At that point, the order becomes a market order and is executed at the best available price. The 320.00 price level cannot be guaranteed. See illustration M–1.

> *Note:* This order can be given as a sell order as well. The significant difference between an MIT order and a Stop order is its location for execution relative to current prices.

*Market-on-Close Order.* An instruction to buy or sell at the best price available during the closing period of the market on a given day. *Also known as:* Market on Close.

*Example:*

Sell 5M May Wheat Market on Close

may also be written as

S 5M K WHT MOC

*Market-on-the-Open Order.* An instruction to buy or sell at the best price available during the opening period of the market on a given day.

*Example:*

Sell 5M May Corn Market on the opening

may also be written as

S 5M K Crn Mkt opening only

Execution can take place only during the exchange-specified opening period. If the market trades in the range of 330 to 335 during that time, any price in that range can be the trade price. Trade price need not be the first price traded nor necessarily be guaranteed to be the best price in that range.

*Margin.* An amount of money deposited by both buyers and sellers of futures contracts to ensure performance of the terms of the contract (the delivery or taking of delivery of the commodity or the cancellation of the position by a subsequent offsetting trade). Margin in commodities is not a payment of equity or down payment on the commodity itself but rather is a performance bond or security deposit.

*Margin Call.* A call from a clearinghouse to a clearing member, or from a brokerage firm to a customer, to bring margin deposits up to a required minimum level.

*Minimum Fluctuation.* The smallest increment or gradation of price movement possible in trading a given contract. *Also known as:* Minimum Price Fluctuation, Point, Tick.

*Example:*

| Commodity | Basis Point Minimum Fluctuation | Dollar Value |
|---|---|---|
| Wheat | 1/4 per bushel | $12.50 |
| Ginnie Mae | 1/32 of a dollar | 31.25 |
| Gold | 10¢ per ounce | 10.00 |
| Cattle | 2 1/2¢ per pound | 10.00 |
| Sugar #11 | 1/100¢ per pound | 11.20 |

*Moving Average.* A method for averaging near-term prices in relation to long-term prices. Oldest prices are dropped as new ones are added.

*Example:*

| Closing prices day 1 | 2.00 |
|---|---|
| 2 | 2.01 |
| 3 | 2.02 |

Average (6.03 divided by 3) = 2.01

As a new day is added, the oldest is dropped.

| Closing prices day 2 | 2.01 |
|---|---|
| 3 | 2.02 |
| 4 | 2.03 |

Average (6.06 divided by 3) = 2.02

*Note:* Moving averages are not restricted to day measurements. Any constant unit measure can be applied, and the average can be of as few as two units to whatever number of units the user wishes.

*Naked Option.* A short option position where the seller does not possess any position in either options or futures that will satisfy exercise of the short option position.

*One-Cancels-the-Other Order.* An order designating both sides or the same side of a trading range with different months, markets, commodities, prices, etc. When the condition of one is reached and executed, the other is canceled.

*Example:*

| |
|---|
| Buy 5M July Soybeans 575 or |
|     5M August         579 One Cancels Other |

may also be written as

| |
|---|
| B 5M N BNS 575 OR 5M Q BNS 579 OCO |

This order may be executed by buying either July or August soybeans. Once either month has been purchased, the other is automatically canceled by the broker. The choice of month traded is left to the broker, who is guided by the dictates of market conditions.

*Open Interest.* The total number of futures contracts of a given commodity that have not yet been offset by opposite futures transactions nor fulfilled by delivery of the commodity; the total number of open transactions. Each open transaction has a buyer and a seller, but for calculation of open interest, only one side of the contract is counted.

*Option Writer.* The seller in an option trade that creates an option contract. The terms ''short'' and ''grantor'' are synonymous with ''writer'' and ''seller.''

*Or-Better Order.* See *Limit Order.*

*Oscillator.* Type of technical analysis tool used in predicting price movements.

*Out Trade.* A trade that does not compare in the clearing process.

*Out-Trade Clerk.* An employee of the clearinghouse charged with helping to resolve problems with unmatched trade confirmations (out trades). The clearinghouse will not recognize a trade (or thus give a trader the desired position) without a matching confirmation enabling the creation of the contra position.

*Pit.* An area of the exchange floor designated for executing orders for a given commodity.

*Premium.* The additional payment allowed by exchange regulations for delivery of higher-than-required standards or grades of a commodity against a futures contract. In speaking of price relationships between different delivery months of a given commodity, one is said to be "trading at a premium" over another when its price is greater than that of the other. In financial instruments, a dollar amount by which a security trades above its principal value.

*Point and Figure Chart.* A chart constructed to detail a continuous flow of price activity without regard to time. Plotting direction is determined by a preset number of price changes in sequential order.

*Price Order.* See *Limit Order.*

*Put Option.* An exchange-traded option contract that gives the purchaser the right, but not the obligation, to enter into an underlying futures contract to be short the commodity at a stated strike price any time prior to the expiration of the option. The grantor of the put has the obligation, upon exercise, to deliver the short futures contract.

*Quote Board.* Mechanism for displaying current prices on commodity futures contracts. The quote board is situated so as to be easily seen from most positions on the trading floor.

*Regression.* Method of statistical analysis that measures quantitative correlations between different variables. One method used to weigh hedges (hedge ratios).

*Relative Strength Indicator.* Technical analysis tool that attempts to indicate when the market has moved excessively in one direction and is likely to be reversed by a technical reversal.

*Round Trip.* See *Round Turn.*

*Round Turn.* The combination of an initiating purchase or sale of a futures contract and the offsetting sale or purchase of an equal number of futures contracts of the same delivery month. Commission fees for commodities transactions cover the round turn.

*Scalper.* An active trader who attempts to profit on small price changes by buying and selling on very short term (current trading day); a floor trader who trades only his/her own account and creates liquidity by buying and selling continuously.

*Seasonality.* Condition of being affected by or occurring during a particular period of the calendar year. This factor determines a repeatable pattern influencing supplies and prices.

*Example:* Price Behavior:

| | Price | |
| --- | --- | --- |
| Commodity | High | Low |
| Wheat | December May | August through September |
| Cotton | July | November through December |

*Short Selling.* Generally, selling something that is not already owned. In futures, a short position not closed out will require the short seller to make delivery of the underlying asset.

*Spot Month.* The near month or current month in which futures trading is still possible and notices can be issued to the long position holder advising that delivery is about to be made. Depending on the commodity, delivery may be the physical commodity or cash settlement in lieu of the commodity.

> *Example:* On the *Chicago Board of Trade* for October Silver:
>
> | | |
> |---|---|
> | *Last Trading Day* | The fourth last business day of the month |
> | *First Notice Day* | Last business day of month preceding the delivery month. |
> | *Last Notice Day* | The next-to-last business day in the delivery month |

*Spread.* The purchase of one futures contract and sale of another, in the expectation that the price relationships between the two will change so that a subsequent offsetting sale and purchase will yield a net profit. Examples include the purchase of one delivery month and the sale of another in the same commodity on the same exchange, or the purchase and sale of the same delivery month in the same commodity on different exchanges, or the purchase of one commodity and the sale of another (wheat vs. corn or corn vs. hogs), or the purchase of one commodity and the sale of the products of that commodity (soybeans vs. soybean oil and soybean meal).

*Standardization.* The uniformity of terms and contract specifications of the futures markets to effectively interface with the cash (spot) markets enabling the transfer of economic risk and recording control (clearance).

*Stochastic—Random.* Finance theorists believing in the efficient market hypothesis hold that futures prices move in a random fashion (stochastic process).

*Stock Index.* A group of stocks selected as representative of the stock market or some industry sector. Changes in the value of the stock index are a way of measuring the changes in the stock market.

*Stock Index Future.* A contract reflecting the value of a selected group of common stocks. Currently, all stock index futures are broad-based indexes reflecting movements of the overall market. These contracts can be used to hedge against or speculate on market moves. There is no physical delivery against any stock index futures. All are cash settlement contracts.

*Stop Order.* See *Limit Order.*

*Straddle (Futures).* Similar to futures spread, a strategy entailing long and short positions in related futures contracts.

*Straddle (Options).* A strategy that entails the purchase (sale) of both calls and puts is known as a long (short) straddle.

*Strike Price.* See *Exercise Price.*

*Supply.* The quantities of a commodity that potential sellers would order for sale at different prices given current conditions. The quantity of commodity supplied is positively related to price.

*Tick Value.* The change in the dollar or cash value of the contract when a futures price changes by the minimum possible price fluctuation (one tick). The tick value is the dollar price equivalent of one tick times the number of units in the futures contract.

> *Examples:* In most grain futures, 1/4¢/bu × 5,000 bu = $12.50, or in 6,000 futures, 10¢/oz × 100 oz = $10.

*Top.* Highest price reached during a market cycle.

*Trade Checking.* The process of reconciling trade confirmations reflecting transactions that have been executed in the trading pits.

*Trading Range.* Range of prices over which market action has been taking place during the time frame under study.

*Volume.* The number of contracts that changed hands during a given period of time.

*Volatility Band.* Range of prices around current market levels that are within the likely trading range.

*Whipsaw.* Term used to describe what has happened to traders that have had stop orders executed as a result of volatile market swings. The traders' intentions were for the stop orders to be executed on market movements indicative of a sustained trend.

# Index